Writing for a **Fast Moving World**

How to Write PROPOSALS, SALES LETTERS & REPORTS

Neil Sawers

Viva Books

New Delhi | Mumbai | Chennai | Kolkata | Bengaluru | Hyderabad | Kochi | Guwahati

First Indian Edition 2009
Reprinted 2011

VIVA BOOKS PRIVATE LIMITED

- 4737/23 Ansari Road, Daryaganj, New Delhi 110 002
  E-mail: vivadelhi@vivagroupindia.net, Tel. 42242200
- 76, Service Industries, Shirvane, Sector 1, Nerul, Navi Mumbai 400 706
  E-mail: vivamumbai@vivagroupindia.net, Tel. 27721273, 27721274
- Jamals Fazal Chambers, 26 Greams Road, Chennai 600 006
  E-mail: vivachennai@vivagroupindia.net, Tel. 28290304, 28294241
- B-103, Jindal Towers, 21/1A/3 Darga Road, Kolkata 700 017
  E-mail: vivakolkata@vivagroupindia.net, Tel. 22836381, 22816713
- 7, Sovereign Park Apartments, 56-58, K. R. Road, Basavanagudi, Bangalore 560 004
  E-mail: vivabangalore@vivagroupindia.net, Tel. 26607409, 26607410
- 101-102 Mughal Marc Apartments, 3-4-637 to 641, Narayanguda, Hyderabad 500 029
  E-mail: vivahyderabad@vivagroupindia.net, Tel. 27564481, 27564482
- Beevi Towers, First Floor, SRM Road, Kaloor, Kochi 682 018, Kerala
  E-mail: vivakochi@vivagroupindia.net, Tel: 0484-2403055, 2403056
- 232, GNB Road, Beside UCO Bank, Silpukhuri, Guwahati 781 003
  E-mail: vivaguwahati@vivagroupindia.net, Tel: 0361-2666386

www.vivagroupindia.com

Published by arrangement with

The NS Group
21 - 10405 Jasper Avenue, Suite 586
Edmonton, AB
Canada
T5J 3S2

ISBN : 978-81-309-1879-2

Published by Vinod Vasishtha for Viva Books Private Limited, 4737/23, Ansari Road, Daryaganj, New Delhi-110 002. Printed and bound by Anand Sons, Delhi-110 092.

CONTENTS

ABOUT THIS BOOK

Purpose and audience

The purpose of Proposals, Sales Letters & Reports is to help you do a better job in working within these three areas. You could be an entrepreneur or owner of a small business. You might be a member of a mid size or large organization. You might be going to college or university and taking some kind of business program. You might also be a student or organization looking for grant funds to assist your particular program or project. This book will help you achieve your objectives.

What this book is designed to accomplish

Each section of this book contains a development process that leads to the writing itself. By working with the process, you put yourself in excellent shape to achieve the writing. As you go through the parts of the book that are most relevant to your needs, you will discover a wealth of information both in the process and in the writing.

How this book is set out

Proposals, Sales Letters & Reports follows the same useful format as that developed for our other book "Ten Steps to Help You Write Better Essays and Term Papers" (ISBN 0-9697901-3-9). The detailed information is on the right page. The left page contains key points as well as scenarios developed to demonstrate real world applications.

"Easy to read, filled with clear concepts and practical examples. This is an excellent introduction for anyone preparing a proposal or report for the first time, and a valuable reference for even the most experienced writers. I intend to keep it close at hand."

Kent Moore, P. Eng.,
Project Management Consultant

ACKNOWLEDGMENTS

Many people have guided me, advised me and contributed to this book. I thank every one of them. In particular I want to thank Gordon W. Banks, Fluidyne Products Inc., Toronto; Ken Cooksley, Calgary; Ray Eliuk, Edmonton; Grant Ericksen, Ericksen Infiniti Nissan, Edmonton; Robert A. Gibbs, Gibbs & Brown Landscape Architects Ltd., Edmonton; Eric Laffoley & Margareta Laffoley, Creative Discovery Ltd., Toronto; Cameron McCleery, McCleery McCann Healthcare, Toronto; Lynne O'Neill, Patrick O'Neill & Elinor Trainer, Extraordinary Conversations Inc., Toronto; Paul Pearson, Arts Development Consultant, Alberta Community Development, Edmonton; Mike Post, Long Beach, CA; Julian Smither, Image Works, Edmonton; Paul A. Wain, CPP, University of Alberta, Edmonton; Brian Wrightson, NAIT, Edmonton.

My final thank you goes to my wife, Marilyn, for wonderful support and a push when needed most.

Proposals

YOUR NOTES

YOUR NOTES

One proposal definition

A written presentation to an individual or organization (the client) to provide your product and/or service to help that client solve a problem or handle a situation.

WHAT IS A PROPOSAL?

Every day, organizations discover that there are things they cannot, or prefer not to, do themselves. They need a product but don't manufacture it; they require a service that is not available in house; they don't have the time, experience or staff to do the job. Sometimes it's an area that is not part of their core business or they have an unworkable situation and need some first-class thinking to resolve it. So they ask someone else to do it for them.

One definition of a proposal is *a written presentation to an individual or organization (the client) to provide your product and/or service or expertise to help that client solve a problem or handle a situation.*

Often project based, proposals cover a broad variety of situations from constructing a building, conducting a customer survey or planning a sales meeting. They can be as simple as a bid to supply lumber, to as complex as producing a television documentary. They are used to apply for a grant to study jazz, or establish a community home care program for seniors. In format, a major RFP (Request for Proposal) with supporting data can run 100 pages or more. On the other hand a small proposal may only be a two or three page letter.

Proposals must be persuasive. You have to convince a client to use you, or, if you're applying for a grant, provide you with funding. Proposals are therefore a selling process.

Structure of the proposal section

I. Types of proposal
II. The discovery process
III. Research & analysis
IV. Your USP (Unique Selling Proposition)
V. Writing up the proposal
VI. Other considerations

This section on proposals deals primarily with how you can best respond to a proposal request. The terms **vendor** and **supplier** used in this section are interchangeable.

Types of proposal

- Request for proposal (RFP)
- Informal
- Speculative
- Grant

I - TYPES OF PROPOSAL

Four types of proposal are considered in this section:

1. *Request for proposal (RFP)*

2. *Informal proposal*

3. *Speculative proposal*

4. *Grant proposal*

In the first two types—RFPs and informal proposals—the client asks for a response to a proposal request. Both are based on a need that the client wishes to resolve and is willing to pay for.

The speculative (sometimes called self-starter) proposal is based on an individual or company seeing a solution to a need or an idea that merits consideration, and trying to sell that solution or idea. The vendor could as easily be a student in college or a major corporation. The vendor approaches the client to find out if the client is (a) interested and (b) willing to fund it.

With grant proposals, a funding agency reviews the requests of individuals or organizations to determine whether they should receive funding for their particular application or project.

The processes in this proposal section, though primarily geared to the first three types of proposal, can be equally valuable in helping individuals and organizations develop their grant applications.

RFP

Client can assess competing submissions

Characteristics

- Formal request
- Specific format
- Larger projects
- Targeted vendors/suppliers
- May short-list best proposals for presentations

Qualifications

May have to:

- Pay fees
- Carry insurance
- Meet location & other operating conditions
- Go through pre-selection process

Must comply with:

- Mandatory requirements

1. REQUEST FOR PROPOSAL (RFP)

What it is

The RFP is a formal request for a proposal from a client to a vendor. The client is usually a major organization, such as government, a university, large corporation, consulting engineer or architect.

Since the RFP is designed to make comparisons based on the same criteria, it allows the client to assess competing proposal applications equally. This is especially true for the provision of services and projects, such as a sales meeting or a construction project, where all vendors must fulfill the same elements. The best proposals received by the client (often three) are usually short-listed, and the vendors invited to make presentations.

RFPs for equipment (often RFQs - Request for Quotation, or Invitations to Tender) are rarely short-listed. Instead, a client evaluation team reviews the submissions and assesses the best overall, based on criteria set out in the RFP/RFQ/Tender.

RFPs tend to be for major projects and equipment with large dollar value. Some projects, such as buildings, highways and infrastructure, require the vendor to pay a fee to obtain architectural drawings, engineering plans or other specifications on which the proposal must be based. This fee tends to restrict applications to serious contenders.

Who gets it?

RFPs go to organizations that the client knows can do the job. An RFP may be open to anyone who can meet the required qualifications. For example, advertisements are placed in local newspapers asking for bids to complete a roadway, construct a building, or repair water and sewer systems. Vendors must demonstrate competencies in the designated areas and are usually required to have insurance coverage.

In addition, many clients now require vendors to go through a pre-selection process. This means that unless you have been cleared beforehand as an approved vendor or supplier by meeting certain standards, you cannot participate.

Mandatory requirements

The RFP requires that all vendors complete their proposal in a specific manner and submit it by a due date and time. It often involves the use of standard forms. Mandatory requirements can include such factors as third party liability insurance, hand delivery to a specific location, or, that submissions by fax are unacceptable.

Ensuring fair bidding

- No vendor identity
- Two envelope process

Evaluation

- May use weighting based on selection criteria

Client briefings

- To clarify information and let vendors ask questions

Making the bid fair

Clients may set up specific requirements to ensure that all vendors have an equal chance. Two practices are:

Anonymous submission. The proposal submitted to the client must be identity free. The vendor's name, or any reference that might identify the vendor, must not appear anywhere, or that vendor will be disqualified. Instead vendors are assigned a number to identify their proposal following evaluation.

Two envelope process. The RFP/client requires each vendor to place everything about the proposal, except price, in one envelope. The price goes in the second envelope. This enables client evaluators to assess a proposal without the possibility of being biased by price.

Evaluation

Many RFPs detail how each submitted proposal will be evaluated, scored and awarded by the client. Selection criteria typically include price, adherence to specifications, references, and abilities demonstrated by past contracts. Each area of the selection criteria will have a weighting established which may be published in the RFP. Many proposals are scored poorly because the vendor fails to provide information specific to the scoring. In any event, a spreadsheet will normally be utilized to compare the various criteria among vendor proposals, whether RFPs or RFQs.

Legal factors

Generally speaking, your response to an RFP is legally an offer. The client can simply accept it and the offer is binding. This reinforces the importance of getting the proposal right and avoiding errors on dollar figures or other factors that can negatively affect you.

Vendors can find RFPs on the Internet

A number of Internet sites now carry listings of RFPs. These listings, by area of interest, such as construction, education and agriculture, give access to many more opportunities. It also means that competition is stiffer and raises questions as to whether you would want to compete.

Briefings

With RFPs involving projects and services, most clients will hold some kind of a briefing, video conference, or conference call to provide additional information or clarification and to allow vendors to ask questions.

Informal proposal

Characteristics

- Less structure than RFP
- Selected vendors
- Client may accept vendors not on list
- Complex/larger proposals usually include a briefing
- Often short-list three best proposals for presentation

A client may send a proposal request to one preferred supplier and not out to bid.

2. INFORMAL PROPOSAL

What it is

An informal proposal is one where a client sends a vendor a proposal package that usually doesn't go into the depth and standardized requirements of an RFP. The package likely details a project that the client wants to have completed. The client invites vendors to submit a proposal on how they would go about it. For example, a bid to supply door frames, a plan to hire call center personnel, a project request to stage a major sales meeting or convention.

Since these informal type proposals are often called requests for proposals, the terms can be confusing.

Who gets the proposal?

Like RFPs, the proposal generally goes out to a small group of organizations known to the client. Sometimes, other interested vendors hear about the proposal and ask to be included. Usually, clients restrict applicants to:

- Those they know can do the job
- A manageable number (they don't want to evaluate dozens of proposals)

The top three project type proposals are usually short-listed, with vendors invited to make presentations. Requests for equipment and supplies, on the other hand, are often evaluated by a client team which then decides where to award the contract.

Informal proposals may not go out to bid. A client may simply go to a preferred supplier and ask them to submit a proposal for a particular project. That supplier still has to submit a bid, but it doesn't need to contain all the information a competitive proposal requires as the client is already well aware of the supplier's capabilities.

Form of proposal package

The proposal package from the client may be a letter, fax, e-mail, or phone call. It may contain enough information so that the vendor can respond with a bid. It often includes an invitation to attend a briefing, especially if the proposal is large or complex.

Speculative proposal

Characteristics

- Self-starter
- Requires proactivity
- Must identify a need
- Existing client the best bet

Important check

- Crunch the numbers—
  is your budget realistic?

Check with the client

- See if client is interested prior to developing a full blown proposal

3. SPECULATIVE PROPOSAL

Not all proposals originate with a request from a client with a need. Sometimes an individual or organization has such a great idea that they look for ways to implement it.

For example, a company might have a new way to recycle plastic, so they'd ask if they could make a proposal to their local government. A group of students might submit a proposal to their student council to hold a concert in the auditorium. These proposals are speculative (sometimes called self-starters).

One potential area for speculative proposals is to a vendor's existing clients. Because you know your client's business so well, you may see areas where improvements might be beneficial. You approach the client to see if they are interested.

Speculative proposals require proactivity

To bring a speculative proposal to reality, companies and individuals have to go out of their way, on their own time and money, to have any chance of success. One industry where speculative proposals are high is film and television where idea pitches are fundamental to generating proposals for documentaries, feature films, or a television series.

Identify a need

The principles behind speculative proposals are no different from other proposals. You must identify a need and come up with a good enough solution to make it worthwhile to a client—whether that be a corporation, a student council, or local authorities.

Have you budgeted and is it realistic?

Have you "crunched" the numbers to make sure that what you are proposing is viable financially? In other words you must be realistic in your assumptions about costs and revenues. You don't want to present anything to a client without being clear what it will cost them, or you.

Is the client interested in what you propose?

There is one very important last point about speculative proposals. Unless you are sure about this proposal, or it's very small and easy to complete, don't spend time doing a full blown proposal without first checking to see if the intended client is sufficiently interested.

Excerpt - speculative proposal

Situation

The city wishes to plant trees along a number of its highways to make the environment more attractive, screen traffic and reduce sound levels. The city would like to accomplish this cost-effectively and with as much eco-sensitivity as possible.

Solution

We propose to supply the city with trees currently growing along power line right of ways. These trees will be harvested by permit from the appropriate authorities, a practice already approved in the past. This is an extraordinarily eco-responsible solution since these trees will normally be cut down, or sprayed with herbicide, to keep the right of way clear.

We select trees of high grade that are of nursery quality (though not of specimen quality since the trees are not pruned).

Cost

These trees are priced more attractively than those from nurseries. We can plant at specified times (best in June or late September) at a cost of $X - $X per tree. (See attached sheet for individual cost by tree type/size.) Larger quantities qualify for reduced rates.

Guarantee

We guarantee these trees to be of good shape. Any tree that does not survive beyond 90 days will be replaced at our cost.

(The segment above is part of a proposal that went to a city government. Permission was given to quote from the proposal. For reasons of confidentiality the client is not identified.)

Check this speculative proposal and mind map

I once helped an associate with a proposal to a small city on providing trees to landscape their local highways. The city had a limited budget. At the same time they wanted to demonstrate that they were good corporate citizens and sensitive to the environment. The proposal we developed would not only save them money, but do it in a remarkably eco-sensitive way. On the opposite page is a segment of the actual proposal.

To help us identify the key points we came up with the mind map shown below. What the mind map did was allow us to develop a simple outline structure to write up the proposal. For more information on the value of using mind maps and other tools for exploration, see pages 36-47.

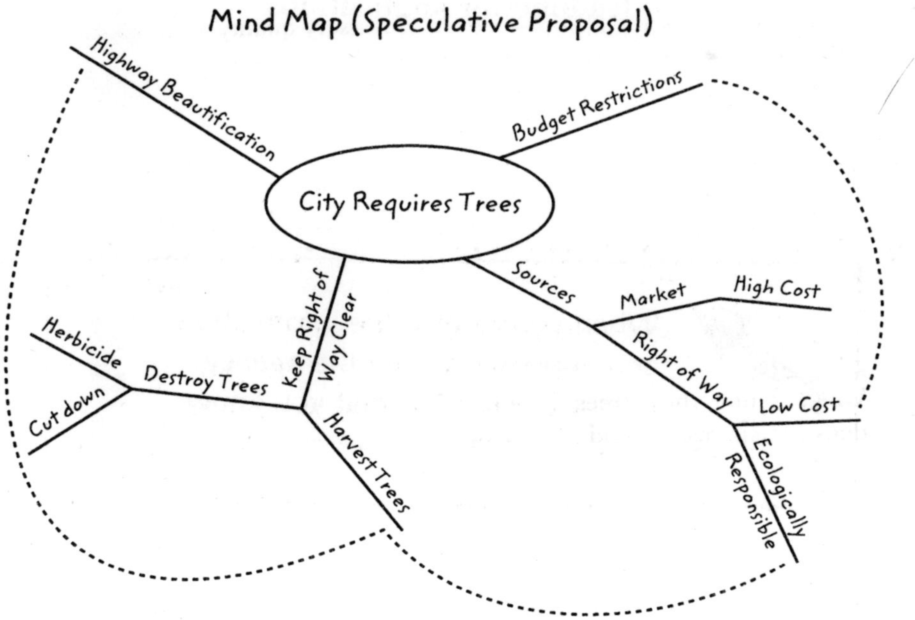

Grant proposal

Characteristics

- Individual/organization looks for suitable granting agency
- Individual/organization must be aware of agency's criteria:
  - eligibility
  - areas considered
  - information required
  - deadline for applications

When you receive the information and application from the agency, read it carefully so that you know what is required.

4. GRANT PROPOSAL

Every year, granting agencies/organizations award millions of dollars in grant monies. These grants, essential to the well being of many individuals and organizations, go to support research and programs in several areas, notably education, health, sports and culture.

Applying for grants has taken on a high level of professionalism, especially at universities and other major research organizations. The focus here is to give those of you who have never applied for a grant before some ideas on how best to go about it.

Applicant

Your job is to:

- Search out agencies who fund the kinds of projects you have in mind
- Obtain an application form
- Write up an effective proposal

Bear in mind that these things can take time. The better you plan what you must do, the more likely you are to succeed.

Agencies

Granting agencies deal in specific areas. Applicants need to know in detail what the agency supports and its rules:

- Who is eligible to apply
- What funding areas will be considered and whether the agency will only match funds first generated elsewhere
- What information they require
- What the deadline is

HOW TO PROCEED

The agency has sent you their application form along with specific information they require you to complete in order to consider your request. Your first job is to carefully read this information so that you are clear about everything the agency requires.

To help your cause:

- Work with the agency
- Use exploration tools
- Avoid any weak elements

You must sell yourself/your organization because reviewers see hundreds of grant applications. What makes your application the one they should choose?

Your cover letter

Can be:

- Acknowledgment of proposal
- Summary of the proposal itself

Before getting into detail, here are three comments to guide you:

1. Work with the agency
2. Use exploration tools
3. Avoid any weak elements

1. *Work with the agency*

Many agencies will help you develop your application, making it much more likely for them to say yes. But you have to be proactive and contact them.

2. *Use exploration tools*

The exploration tools described on pages 36-47 are valuable in the development of RFPs, informal and speculative proposals. These tools—your own thinking, brainstorming, mind mapping and freewriting—can be equally valuable if you have a grant proposal to prepare.

3. *Avoid any weak elements*

Each part of the proposal must be prepared equally well. You do not want a reviewer to turn down your request because of one weak area.

IT'S A SELL JOB

It may sound crass but this is a sell job, just like every other proposal. Every year, hundreds of less worthy applications are approved over others that are much more deserving. The only difference is the ability to complete a winning application. So remember this—reviewers wade through hundreds of applications. Your job is to make it easy for them to choose yours.

So, what do they want to see? Here are the components:

Cover letter

The cover letter may simply be an acknowledgment of the attached proposal and a thank you to the agency for their consideration. In some proposals, especially smaller ones, the cover letter may be a summary of the proposal itself.

Summary

- Brief compelling recap

Core application elements

YOU/YOUR ORGANIZATION

- Your achievements
- What makes you special?

WHAT PROJECT IS ABOUT

Individual

- Commitment to profession
- Demonstrated talent
- Qualifications

Organization

- Commitment to project/program
- Reputation
- Qualifications

Summary

This page contains a recap of your proposal. Keep it short, preferably two to three paragraphs. It must be compelling enough for the application to receive serious consideration.

Core of the application

The core elements of the grant application include:

- Who you are as individual or organization
- What your project is about
- Why there is a need for this project
- How you plan to carry it out
- Your budget
- How you will evaluate the project
- How it relates to the agency's objectives
- Testimonials/endorsements

The sequencing of these elements can vary. If you are applying to pursue dance studies, for example, your application will focus first on who you are as an individual. With an organization, it's more likely to begin with what you want to do, such as develop a home care program.

Who you are as individual or organization

This section deals with who you are. What have your achievements been? What is your track record? With whom have you been associated in your career? If you are an organization, the same type of criteria apply. What has your organization achieved? Who are the people involved and their credentials? What makes your organization special?

What your project is about

This is the key element. For an individual requesting a grant, it must say something about you and your commitment to your writing, craft, performing profession—talent that you have already demonstrated. Reviewers want to know your passion and commitment to your objectives

For organizations, it's the particular project or program the organization wishes to present, its qualifications to do so and the difference it will make. Will this benefit the community? Will it support health or cultural programs, or the domain in which the organization operates?

PROJECT NEED/IMPORTANCE

- Justify the need
- Supporting data

HOW YOU WILL CARRY IT OUT

- Actions to be taken
- Can project be completed:
  - with this grant?
  - in this time frame?
- Is other funding required to complete it? If so, is it in place?

YOUR BUDGET

- Provide detail
- Be realistic
- Track your expenditures

EVALUATION

- Must be measurable
- Compare before and after

Why there is a need for this project

For an individual, can you communicate to the reviewer why this grant is important? For example, it could make a difference to your growth and the advancement of your career. It's one more step to achieve your goals.

For an organization, why do you want to build this theater, provide home care programs, support a choral singing program for teenagers? Are you able to define the need? What data do you have to back up your claim? Demographics? Demand from other agencies? Use the exploration tools to help you build your case.

How you plan to carry it out

This is the action step and it details the stages in which you plan to carry out your project, whether that's taking an advanced dance class or renovating a recreation facility. Is it all to be completed in one year, or spread over a number of years? If the latter, how do you plan to finance the completion of the project? Agencies like assurance that your project will be completed, whether they provide the funding or it comes partly from elsewhere.

Your budget

Agencies want to know, in sufficient detail, what you expect your costs to be. So for each element of the project, each stage, those costs should be set out in as much detail as possible. Don't inflate your costs, or, conversely, under budget yourself. Be realistic. You will be required to justify your expenses and keep track of what you spend.

How you will evaluate the project

Will it be worth it? Both agency and recipient need to reflect on whether the grant was a good use of agency funds. It's important, therefore, before the grant gets under way, to establish how the results will be measured and over what time frame. A good starting point is understanding the present situation—then, at the end of the funding period, identifying what has been achieved in relation to the objective. Did you renovate your recreation facility? Did you establish your home care program? Is your novel ready for publication?

RELATIONSHIP TO AGENCY'S OBJECTIVES

- Does your application fit with why the agency is in business?

ENDORSEMENTS/TESTIMONIALS

- Credible
- Authoritative
- Professional

Technical check

- Keep it short - preferably 2-3 pages
- Keep it simple (KISS principle)
- Be specific
- Use:
  - one side of paper
  - double spaced
  - wide margin
- Grammar/spelling flawless
- Serif font (easier to read)

Keep your application:

- Tight and crisp
- High on specifics, low on generalities

Reviewers are experts in their field. They are rarely fooled.

How this project/request relates to agency objectives

Agencies are in business because they strongly believe that what they are doing is worthwhile and makes a difference. It is therefore a wise move to support the agency by stating how your request or project meets the agency's objectives.

Endorsements/Testimonials

Reviewers look for credibility. Endorsements and testimonials come best from independent and professional sources. For example, if you propose to renovate a building to support concerts and dance performances, it would be very helpful to have endorsement by your local city council as well as the performing organizations who would benefit. If you're a writer, testimonials from editors, other professionals and instructors should be included in your application.

TECHNICAL CHECK

When preparing your grant application, keep the following in mind:

a. Remember the KISS principle—keep it simple
b. Check for grammar and spelling
c. Use one side of paper only, double spaced
d. Use a serif font (like this one). It's easier to read
e. Keep a wide left hand margin. A reviewer can then write in the margin. Since it makes the overall column narrower, your application is often an easier read

Reviewers will not waste their time on applications that are too complex, short on detail, lacking clarity, or too long. They don't want to see an individual application longer than 2 to 3 pages. Applications from organizations, which are likely to be longer, should be kept as tight and crisp as possible. Reviewers expect applications to be high on specifics and low on generalities. Too many that fail are the reverse.

One final point. Applicants are sometimes under the impression that their application will be reviewed by agency or government bureaucrats who are unfamiliar with the areas involved. This misconception often leads to applicants exaggerating either their experience or the project. Be aware that reviewers are chosen because of their expertise in their field. They are rarely fooled.

Types of proposal - summary criteria

	RFP	Informal	Speculative	Grant
Information package	Yes	Yes	No	Yes
Briefing	Yes	Often	No	No
Endorsement/ Testimonials	Yes	Yes	Yes	Yes
Specific forms	Yes	No	No	Yes
Deadline	Yes	Yes	No	Yes
No. of bidders	Limited	Limited	Anyone	Anyone
Request	Formal/ Legal	Formal/ Informal	Informal	Semi-formal
Format	Specific	Specific/ Your choice	Your choice	Specific
Fees required	Maybe	Maybe	No	No
Short-list	Yes	Yes	No	No

Summary of proposal criteria

The four types of proposals and the criteria that belong to each one are summarized on the opposite page. No hard and fast rules exist here. Just because no briefing shows up under speculative proposal doesn't mean there definitely won't be a briefing. If the potential client likes the idea, some kind of meeting will certainly be held.

An informal proposal to plan a major sales meeting may in fact be a whole lot more formal in its overall handling by the client than some RFPs. What is generally true is that informal and speculative proposals are more flexible than RFPs and grant proposals.

Make sure you get value from the rest of the proposal section

Every single proposal can benefit from the information in the remainder of the proposal section. Even those parts dealing with research and your USP (Unique Selling Proposition), though less likely to be required for grant proposals, can have value.

Next steps

Whether you are completing an RFP, informal proposal, speculative or grant proposal, your job is to convince those requesting the proposal, or those providing funds, that:

- *Your proposal is the best*
- *You are the right person/organization for the job*

The discovery process will help you do that.

The discovery process

Your objective

- Understand the client's present position
- Be clear on what the client wants to achieve
- Be aware of any factors that may impact the proposal

Take the time to do the up-front work...the fact finding, research, knowledge and intelligence you must bring to bear to achieve the objectives set out above.

II - THE DISCOVERY PROCESS

The discovery process is arguably the most important part of developing proposals. The end result of this process is that you:

- Fully understand the client's present position
- Are totally clear on what the client wants to achieve
- Are aware of any special factors that may impact the proposal

The discovery process is all about the importance of doing the up-front work. This work involves the fact finding, research, knowledge and intelligence that you bring to bear in order to achieve the above results. Integral parts of this up-front work are:

- The use of exploration tools
- The proposal package itself
- Any briefing you attend

First, however, I want to stress why this up-front work is so important.

Importance of the up-front work

Too many vendors fail to get the order because they don't spend enough time up front to do the information gathering, research work and analysis critical to fully understanding what must go into a proposal.

Let me show you what I mean by using two different approaches. We'll assume that you're bidding on catering a dinner for a quarterly staff meeting at a medium-sized company.

First approach

You sit down with the client, discuss the kind of meal they want, the number of people and the budget. Equipped with this information, you come up with your proposal. The client thanks you, and says they'll get back to you.

The up-front work leads to clear focus and direction

Regular triangle (1st approach)

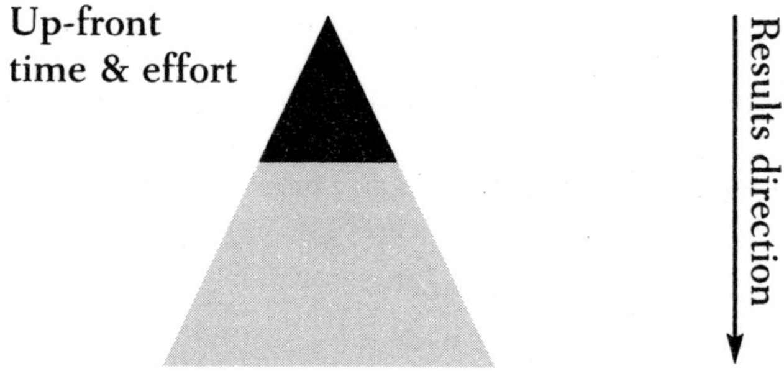

Scattered focus =
too little work up front

Inverted triangle (2nd approach)

Focused result =
successful work up front

To a large degree, discovery is all about asking questions.

Second approach

You sit down with the client and start to ask some questions. For what kind of occasion is this meal? Is there anything special the client wants to achieve? You discover that this is the firm's fifth year in business, and because they're doing well, this is more of a celebration.

By probing deeper you find out that two people will be specially honored. One is leaving to take up another position after making substantial contributions to the company. The other is being promoted to fill the vacancy. The company is also celebrating the introduction of a new product to the market.

In your proposal, you tailor the meal to the occasion—you know exactly what it is the client wants to achieve. The client accepts your proposal.

The triangle graphic on the opposite page illustrates both approaches.

The ***regular triangle*** represents the ***first approach***.
See how little time was spent at the top to discover the real situation. Many vendors make this mistake. They want to get to the proposal so badly, especially their ideas to solve the problem, that they spend insufficient time up front to make sure they are aware of all the ramifications. As the triangle demonstrates, they are not focused on the result. This approach fails.

The ***inverted triangle*** represents the ***second approach***.
Time is taken to find out, up front, what the client really wants. As a result the vendor is focused on the client's desired result. This approach succeeds.

Yes, it's a simple illustration, but here's the point. When you're clear on what the client needs, because you've done the up-front work to find out, you are properly focused on finding the solution.

Discovery is all about ***asking questions*** and setting the big problem front and center so it can be examined—and questioned again. One approach is to focus first on the negative—on what may not be working—then move on to the positive solution.

Use exploration tools

Your own thinking
Brainstorming
Mind mapping
Freewriting (Rapidwriting)

These tools help in:

- Research planning
- Briefing and proposal preparation

Importance of inclusion

The more you involve your team and other associates in using these tools, the greater the input and the better the results.

USE EXPLORATION TOOLS

These tools and concepts will help you do research invaluable in preparing for a briefing, as well as deciding how best to approach the proposal itself. You are probably familiar with these tools, but do you use them? They are:

- Your own thinking
- Brainstorming
- Mind maps
- Freewriting (or Rapidwriting)

These tools take advantage of the way our minds work. We don't think linearly. Rather we think in random patterns, with diverse thoughts and ideas. Mind mapping in particular allows all those thoughts to surface, then be placed in an orderly sequence.

Importance of inclusion

In working with these tools, be sure that everyone's opinion is both requested and respected. This is particularly important in techniques such as brainstorming and mind mapping. Sometimes the most outrageous thoughts and ideas lead to powerful answers or solutions, or ways to proceed.

Landscape scenario

Throughout the rest of this section on proposals, we have created a scenario to help illustrate not just these exploration tools, but the entire proposal process. It is this:

You are a landscape architect. You are one of a number of vendors who have been asked to respond to a proposal request from a developer, Western Associates, to provide landscape design for a park in a major, new housing development called Glen Arran Estates. You have received the proposal package with budget details. There's a briefing the day after tomorrow.

Your own thinking

Landscape Scenario

Is their budget realistic?

I need to see the site itself to get a better picture.

How big is it, what shape's it in? Are there any trees?

Will the general public be using this area or is access only available to residents?

How close is this to the highway? Is it noisy?

The southeast section—is the client concerned that resolving the water issue to meet both environmental needs and limit flooding will cost too much?

How quickly do they want to proceed to site construction? Can we do something special or is this a rush job? This client has a reasonable reputation—we haven't worked with them before—wonder who has and if we can find out.

Brainstorming rules

- Write down every idea
- No censorship
- No judgment
- No evaluation
- No editing

Evaluate each idea. Keep those that might contribute to your proposal. Group items into categories to help you plan and set priorities.

Your own thinking

It's very easy to rush into a project without giving yourself a chance to sit back and look at the implications. I suggest that you relax and think of what this proposal about. In particular, try to understand what the client is thinking.

Take breaks to collect your thoughts. It doesn't have to be at the office—it can be down at the coffee shop, taking a walk—the choices are yours. Do it alone, do it with your team, but do it. And keep a notebook or electronic organizer with you, to write down any thoughts or ideas so they're not forgotten. On the page opposite is what I came up with in thinking about the Landscape Scenario.

Brainstorming

Brainstorming is a freewheeling session, by yourself or with others, in which you focus on the area you wish to examine. You let every idea about the issue come up, and, no matter how farfetched it seems, you write it down.

Start with a sheet of paper, flip chart or computer screen. If two or three of you are working together, have one person act as recorder to write everything down.

While brainstorming, check do's and don'ts:

- Do write down each idea, each thought, one after the other, wherever it comes from
- Don't censor yourself or anyone else
- Don't evaluate or judge anything

Once the ideas are down:

- Evaluate what you've got
- Eliminate those ideas that don't work
- Highlight those with the most potential and incorporate them into the information you are collecting

Once you've done this you can group items which fit together into categories to help you plan and set priorities.

Brainstorming is a great way to keep this freewheeling, thinking process on the move. Combining it with mind maps, however, can really make a difference.

Traditional mind map

1. Take a sheet of paper, a whiteboard, or flip chart. In the middle write down the topic. i.e. landscaping.
2. Every thought, every idea about that topic goes down on the paper as branches on a map.
3. Each branch represents similar thoughts or ideas. Any new thought or idea pertaining to an existing branch is added to that branch.
4. A totally new idea receives a branch of its own.

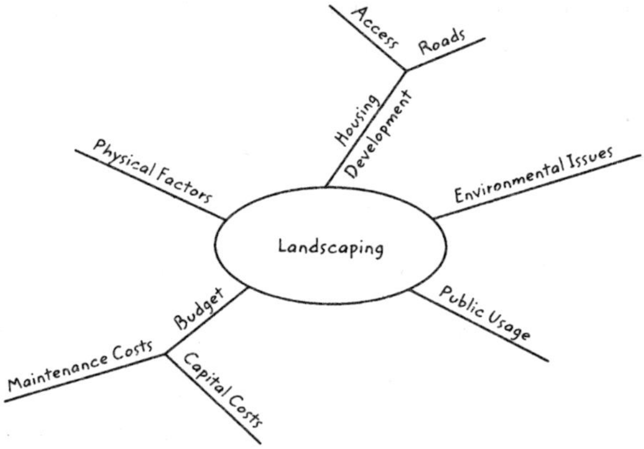

Self-stick notes mind map

1. Write the issue on a self-stick note and place it at the top of the surface you're using
2. The main branch headings now head up columns in a line underneath the issue, like an organization chart.
3. Every thought and idea should be written on a self-stick note and placed below the column to which it pertains.
4. Create a new column if it's a different area altogether.

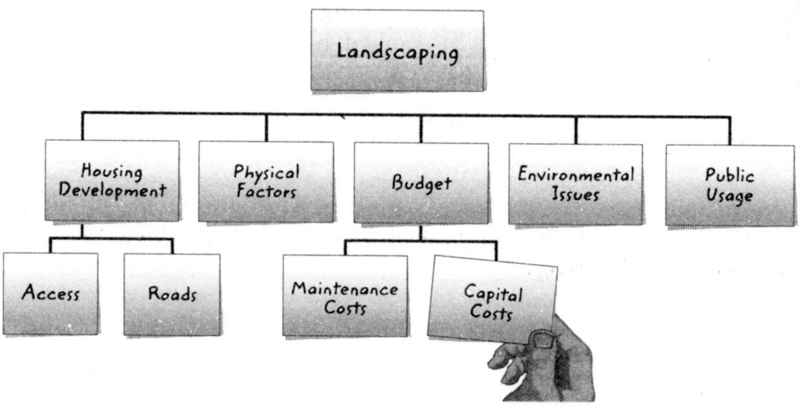

Mind maps®

Making a mind map, or mind mapping, is one of the most valuable tools I have ever come across (variations of this process are ***branching*** and ***clustering***). You can use mind mapping for just about any planning or thinking—your vacation, developing your garden, and of course proposals, sales letters and reports.

There are two approaches to mind mapping—the traditional approach, and using self-stick notes, such as 3M's Post-it® Notes. Both approaches are shown on the opposite page.

Traditional approach

The top box on the opposite page sets out how to develop a traditional mind map. The end result is rather like looking at a tree from above. So far, five main branches relating to the landscaping topic, have been identified. They are housing development, physical factors, budget, public usage and environmental issues. The branches give order and flow to your thoughts and ideas. You often notice connections between the branches. As the mind map expands, these connections become more apparent and priorities start to show up. This is very useful in helping you analyze what you're working on.

Using self-stick notes

You need a surface, such as a wall, window, or flip chart. I like flip charts because they're flexible and the paper size allows for lots of space, very helpful when using self-stick notes. The lower box on the page opposite explains how to develop a self-stick notes mind map.

Now here's what's valuable about self-stick notes. The unique quality of the product lets you:

- ***Move a self-stick note around***. If something doesn't fit in one column and belongs in another, you can move it there.
- ***You can assess priorities***. When reading down a column and it's clear that one item should be ranked higher than another, you simply move it up or down.

On the next two pages you can see what happens with these two approaches as more details are added.

Mind Maps® is a Registered Trademark of the Buzan Centres - used here with enthusiastic permission.

Traditional Mind Map

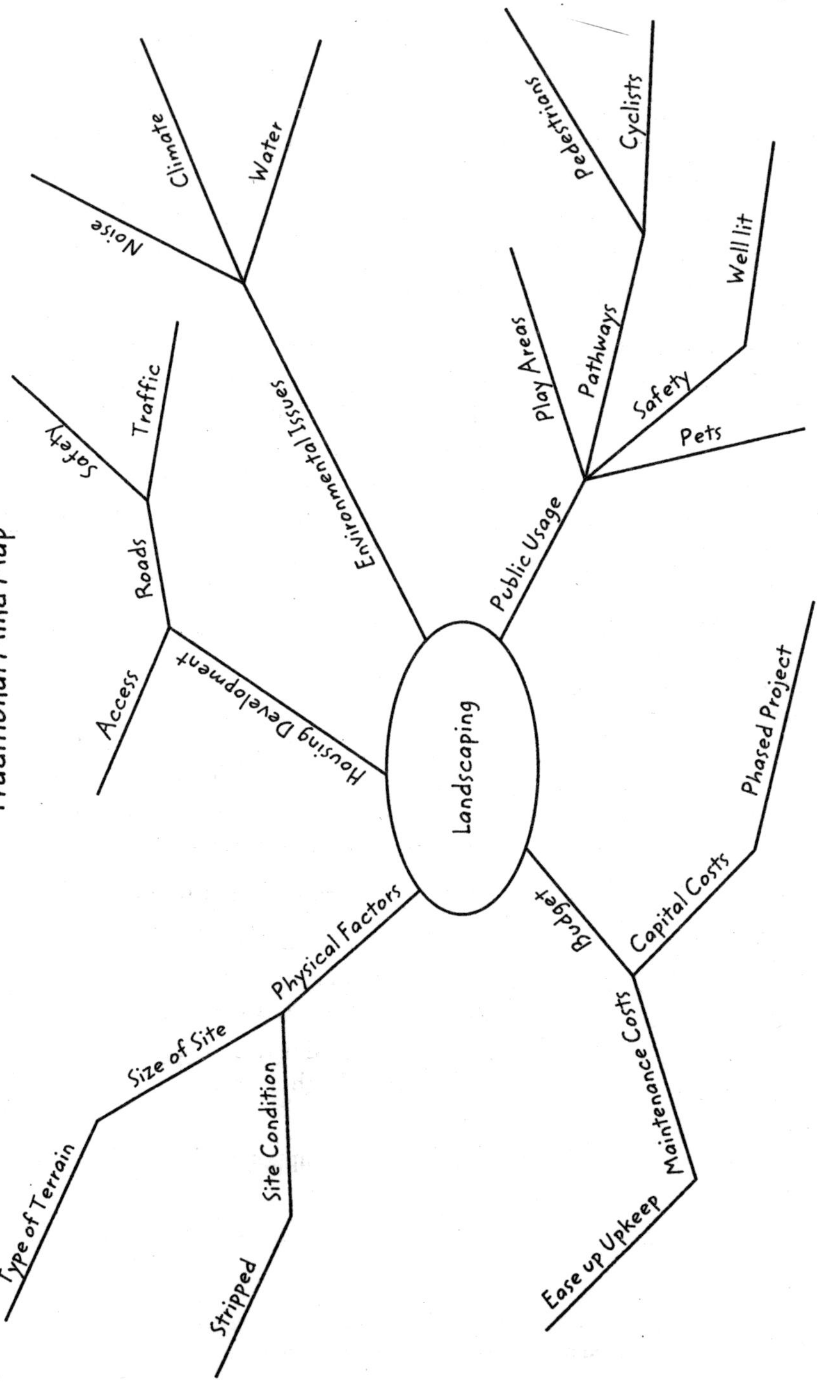

Self-stick Notes Mind Map

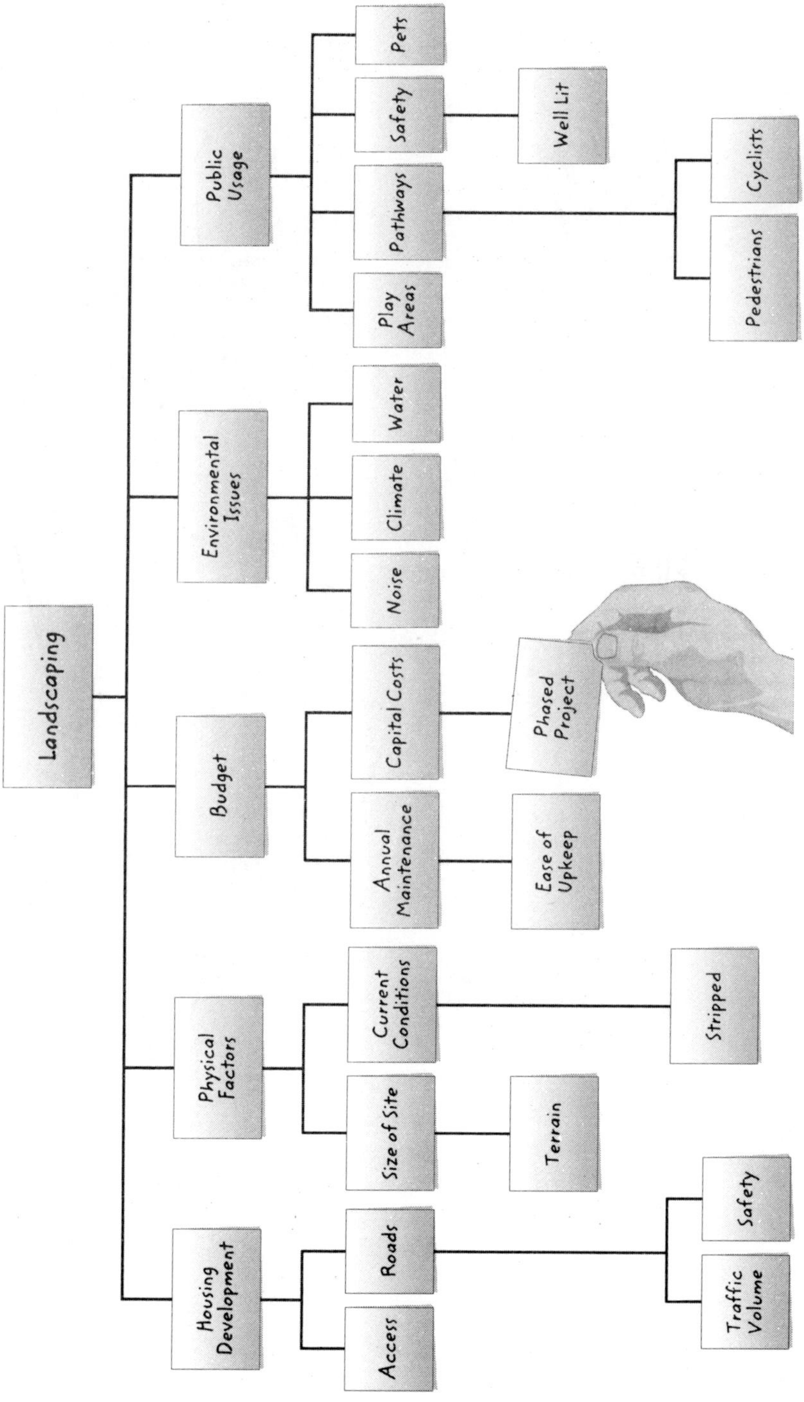

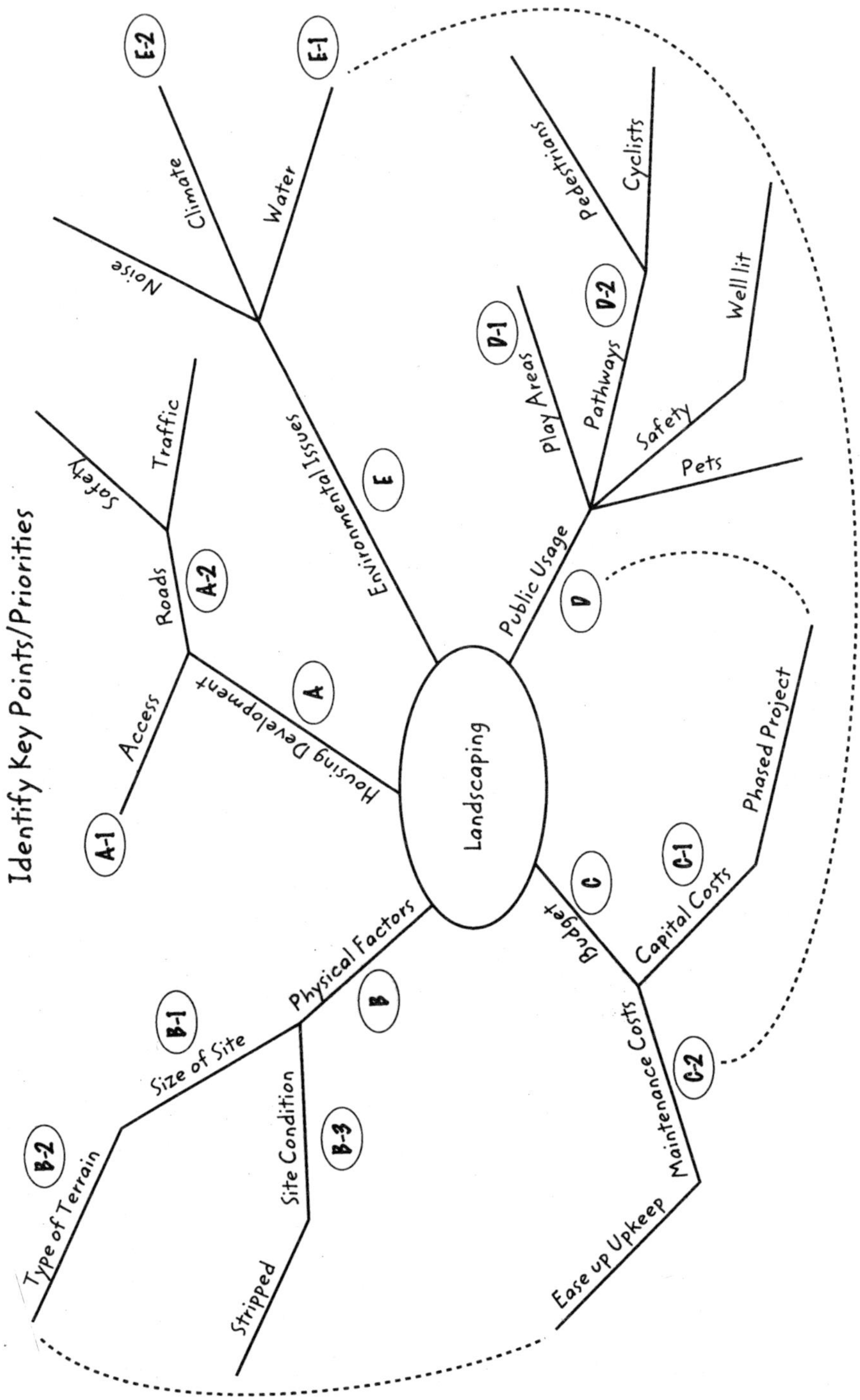
Identify Key Points/Priorities
Landscaping
Housing Development
A
Access
A-1
Roads
A-2
Safety
Traffic
Environmental Issues
E
Noise
Climate
E-2
Water
E-1
Public Usage
D
Play Areas
D-1
Pathways
D-2
Pedestrians
Cyclists
Safety
Well lit
Pets
Budget
C
Capital Costs
C-1
Phased Project
Maintenance Costs
C-2
Ease up Upkeep
Physical Factors
B
Size of Site
B-1
Type of Terrain
B-2
Site Condition
B-3
Stripped

Mind map analysis

Once the information is down, analyze what you've got. Look for patterns. How does one branch (or column if you use self-stick notes) relate to another? What bridges could you create? What conclusions could you draw? In my experience, when you create a mind map, the important things seem to jump out at you.

A mind map can help identify alternative courses of action, their advantages and disadvantages. It can tell you where you're light or heavy on the work you've done. Do you need to spend more time in one area and less in another?

Identify the priorities

A mind map can be extraordinarily useful in identifying key points, or priorities. It will help you determine the kinds of things you want to cover or find out in a briefing.

When it comes to developing the proposal itself, numbering the priorities can give you the natural, step by step, linear outline to set out your material. In the Landscape Scenario, we have numbered the priority areas A through E, with A-1, B-1 and so on detailing subheadings under each priority. Here's the likely sequence for discussing the current situation together with the client's objectives:

A. Status of the development itself. How many people reside there? What about the roads?

B. How big is the site? What's there now? What's the terrain? Flat? Hilly? What about soil or vegetation?

C. The client desires an attractive new environment. There are reasonable dollars for initial capital costs, but the client wants annual maintenance costs to be minimal

D. Full public usage of the area is desirable

E. Environmental and safety factors must be observed

Freewriting

- Just write
- Give yourself a time frame
- Don't censor yourself
- Highlight new key points

Landscape Scenario: **Five minute freewrite**

Just thinking about this proposal. What general direction is the site facing? Is there a lot of sun into the area? Does it face west? People like to have sunlight at the end of the day. Now it would be useful if we surveyed any of the people who have moved into the development and find out what they would like to see. They're going to be using it. Do they want more pedestrian areas? Do they want a skateboard area for their kids? Reminds me—do we know the demographic? Is this a development which will attract lots of kids? How much should we prepare for them?

What do we do about water? I've been told that it may be a problem in the southeast area—there's a stream there and if we get heavy rain it tends to flood. Apparently the contractors had to watch that during construction of the homes. There's some thought that the environment people will want to protect the stream because it's rated a wetlands habitat. Will have to watch for that one. Who would we use to guide us on that one?

Back to the park—what kind of seating areas, or covered protected areas might they like? Should we have areas for dogs or not? Dogs are messy as owners frequently don't pick up after their animals.

Should we plan for drinking water fountains or is that too much of a problem? We don't want to make more problems and more maintenance than necessary.

Is there something imaginative we can do with trees? Like many developments, this hasn't many trees left—I don't think there were that many to start with—what would be a good mix of deciduous and evergreen?

Freewriting

Freewriting (or Rapidwriting) is similar to brainstorming in that you write down everything that comes into your head. The difference is that you can write down anything you want—insights, comparison of ideas, criticism of ideas, any judgments you want to make in the moment. Nothing is barred. Just write.

I've done this many times and it's remarkable what can come forth if you're prepared to remove self-imposed limitations and think ***outside of the box***.

Rules for freewriting:

- Give yourself a time frame—it might be five minutes, 15 minutes, half an hour—and just write about the area you're dealing with
- Don't stop writing—just let the words and ideas flow
- Don't censor yourself, say this is no good, or correct anything

When your time is up, stop, then examine what you've written. You may be amazed at the wealth of information that can be generated from this simple exercise.

Take a highlighter and highlight the key points. If this is new information, add it to your mind map or whatever method you are using to organize your work.

When to use exploration tools

Exploration tools are valuable at any stage of the proposal process, from understanding the present situation, getting prepared for briefings, doing research, and, as you will discover, for writing the proposal itself.

Up-front information sources

The proposal package details:

- Situation
- What client needs
- Budget
- Timeline

Check the numbers

Use a spreadsheet to test any preliminary calculations against the client's budget. Can you work with it?

Briefings

- Client provides vendors with more information
- Vendors can ask questions and clarify any issues or concerns

UP-FRONT INFORMATION SOURCES

The two main areas of direct information are:

- The proposal package
- Briefings

The proposal package

The package supplied by the client provides you with the basic information; i.e. here's the situation, here's what we want, here's the budget and deadline. Sometimes everything you need to know is included in the package. All you have to do is develop your approach and submit your proposal. If you have questions you simply contact the client for answers or clarification.

Things are not usually that simple, however. If the proposal is at all complex, there will likely be a briefing.

Check the numbers

Assuming you know the client's budget, it makes very good sense to do some preliminary checking on costs, based on a possible solution to the client's needs.

This is one of the very important pieces of up-front work. Based on the results, you may decide to compete on the proposal, or decline the opportunity. A method many companies apply is to use a spreadsheet template to test a model. They plug in the client's budget figures and match these against the cost estimates of their model. If you do this at an early stage, you can determine whether the client's budget figures seem realistic. Vendors sometimes get in trouble because they jump straight to their solution without first doing any calculations.

Briefings

Briefings can be formal or informal. They may take place with all vendors in the room or via videoconferencing or conference call. They might also take place one on one, in person or by phone.

You hear directly from the client what the objectives are and the issues they face. You have the opportunity to ask questions and get those questions answered.

Pre-briefing

Preparation

- Review proposal package with your team
- What questions does it raise?

Landscape Scenario:

Questions about the project might be...

Is your company willing to look at additional capital cost expenditures if it can be shown that these expenditures will significantly reduce annual maintenance costs?

Is access to the park for residents only or can it be used by the general public? If so, what are the implications?

Research the client on:

- Issues they face
- Shape of their industry

Impress the client on:

- Quality of your research
- Your interest in working with them

Landscape Scenario: **Your client knowledge**

We understand that in a couple of previous projects Western Associates encountered some problems in overcoming environmental concerns. Our company has an excellent reputation in this area—environment department personnel have commended our approach in situations similar to the flooding/wetlands issues faced at Glen Arran Estates.

Pre-briefing

Come to the briefing well prepared

Read through the proposal package several times with your team so that you:

- Have an appreciation of what the client wants
- Are aware of what the proposal will entail
- Avoid misunderstandings
- Know what questions to ask in terms of clarification, issues raised, budgets and timelines

Any research you do will depend on the kind of information you need—about the market, about the competition, concerning any ideas you have, or plans you think will work for the client. Use exploration tools like brainstorming or mind mapping to help you.

Research the client

Make sure you do sufficient research on the client, even if you've worked with them before. Who are they? What business are they in? What are their expectations? Who are their key players? Who are the decision makers? What kinds of issues are they facing? In the industry? In the economy?

The more you can demonstrate your knowledge of the client's business, the more impressed they are likely to be about your ability to do the job, even before they receive your proposal. This kind of research has two major benefits:

1. You get a better understanding of the situation and therefore the potential solution
2. You develop a positive relationship—clients generally appreciate those who make the extra efforts to serve them and are more likely to want to work with them

Take key people to the briefing with you

If the proposal requires a team, such as for a major sales meeting, decide what kinds of skills you need on that team and assemble it. Then, if possible and practical, take these people to the briefing.

Take key people to the briefing

- Everyone hears the same thing
- Specialist team members can ask and answer key questions
- You build relationships with the client

Give the client added value

- Provide useful extra information and/or research

During the briefing

Listen and ask the right questions

- Listen for clarity
- Get all questions answered

> Landscape Scenario
>
> *Some typical questions on finding out where a client "sits" in terms of relationship may be appropriate during a briefing:*
>
> Have you worked with other suppliers like us before? How was that experience—and what are you looking for in terms of a relationship?

Avoid assumptions

- Assume nothing!
- Clarify issues by feeding back to the client what you thought you understood. They'll correct you if necessary

The benefits of having team members present include:

Everyone hears from the client first-hand
If it's just you at the briefing, you may miss some element of the picture. Colleagues can raise important issues or questions you might not have considered. As well, the whole team has a chance to appreciate the client scenario—you're all on the same wavelength.

Building relationships with the client
Some proposals with which I've been involved were won as much by relationship as by merit. If two proposals are equally good and the chemistry with one firm is better than with another, the client chooses the one with whom they are more comfortable.

Bring added value to the table

Find a way to go farther, proactively, to assist the client. I once did some research on identification systems to give us a better handle on a video the client wanted for their new card ID system. This additional effort surprised the client and gave us extra credibility. In what way could you add value for the client?

During the briefing

Listen and ask the right questions

It's an obvious point perhaps, but important. When you take the time to listen to what the client has to say, you don't miss critical information. At the same time, ask the questions that came out of your pre-briefing planning to get clear on any issues. By the questions you ask and your knowledge of their business, the client will appreciate that you have done your homework.

Be careful with assumptions

I was once involved in a proposal to a major brewer. The briefing had come from the company's human relations officer and an outside consultant. We were at least one step removed from the president who was the decision maker, a situation I never like to be in. Our proposal was based on information from the briefing, which we later discovered was incomplete. Since the proposal failed to reflect what the client actually needed, it was rejected.

Assume nothing. Check your assumptions. Reflect back to the client what you ***thought*** you heard (or saw, or read) and whether it's accurate. The client will either concur, or correct your impression.

Confirm the budget

- If you don't know the budget, try to get the client to come up with an acceptable figure
- Give the client options if useful and appropriate

Who makes the decision?

Do those giving the briefing make the decision? If not, find out who does.

Know what the budget is

The RFP or proposal package will usually tell you what the budget is, or at least give a range. Obviously this is not true if the proposal is a low price bid on some lumber. In other circumstances the client might act as follows:

- They don't give a budget but say they have a "ballpark" figure in mind
- They ask what it would cost to do something (especially if you are the preferred supplier and there are no other vendors)
- They ask you to bid based on the information given

Let's say that a client comes to you and asks "Give us some idea of what it will cost to do X?" You estimate a figure you believe to be reasonable. If the client doesn't accept it, you have to find out what monies the client has in mind. A colleague uses a tactic like "Well is it as high as $100,000?" "No." "How about as low as $60,000?" "No." They edge towards numbers, going high and low, until some acceptable figure is reached.

Options

The client may be willing to look at options:

- What you could do for the budget dollars
- Break a project into phases:
  - we could do Phase 1 now for $25,000
  - we could do Phase 2 in six months for $35,000

Know the decision maker/s

I have been to briefings where we were assured that those providing the briefing would also be making the decision. Except it wasn't true. My experience is that knowing who the decision maker is almost always makes a difference. You know who you're dealing with. As well, make sure you know the decision maker's perspective on the proposal by checking with them to see if it agrees with that of other client staff.

Ongoing access to the client

Who do you contact if you need further information or clarification?

Competitive bid?

Is the winner the vendor with the best proposal or a client going through the motions to satisfy legal or corporate requirements? Try to find out.

Ongoing access to the client

If you're working on the project and need answers, where do you get them? Obviously you need to know who to contact if you have further questions after a briefing, or if there is no briefing. In my experience, clients are quite willing, within reason, to take the time to answer any questions you may have. To make it easier on their staff, however, they may require questions to be channeled through one person or department.

If you can get a personal meeting with key players, do so. If you can't do it in person, phone them. If you cannot get them by phone, e-mail them. They will usually respond. There's one very important point—the questions must be short and relevant to the proposal.

A word of caution. One of the conditions of a proposal might be that you may only go through the designated contact. If you have contacted other client personnel your proposal might be rejected—unless all competing vendors received equal access.

Is this a competitive bid?

Some organizations are required in their by-laws to ask for competitive bids, although they intend to give the contract to a particular vendor (who has worked well for them).

A production company I worked with received a request from a blue chip company to stage a half million dollar sales event. Several other vendors were invited. Some spent thousands of dollars to make their proposal.

Turns out that the blue chip company was happy with the vendor they'd used in the past and planned to give them the contract all along. They simply had to satisfy their legal requirements.

Try to find out whether the successful vendor will be the one with the best proposal, and not awarded by some other rationale.

Post-briefing

Ask yourself:

- Does this proposal:
  - interest you?
  - reward you enough?
  - interfere with other objectives?
- Can you:
  - meet the deadline?
  - work with this client?
- Are you qualified?

Consider declining if the answers are negative

The exception
Where a proposal offers a great opportunity to your career path

Plan the proposal with your team

- Discuss:
  - scope and issues
  - who should be involved
  - research to be done
  - budget
  - deadlines

Post-briefing

You and your team get together to decide the next steps.

Do you want to do this proposal?

I wish I'd turned down one project where the budget was far too small. We ended up donating thousands of dollars worth of time and effort that would have been better spent elsewhere. Consider turning down a proposal request if:

- It's not an area that interests you
- It's too costly or there's insufficient reward
- It will take up too much time or the deadline's impossible to meet
- There are simply too many competitors (one of whom may well be a preferred supplier)
- You're not qualified

This last point is very important in legal terms. You have to assess risk here in terms of liability. Are you confident that you are qualified to do the job and are willing to sign a contract to that effect?

You can decide not to make a bid based on any number of reasons, including those above. On the other hand, a proposal can provide a tremendous opportunity to learn and take you where you want to go on your career path. If that's the case, it may be worth going for.

Plan the proposal

You've decided to make a bid. Now you have to plan the work. Involve the team and bring everyone up to speed so that they can do the best possible job in their own areas. Questions to consider are:

- How big is the proposal?
- What areas does it encompass?
- How many people will it require?
- Will it need other specialized team members?
- How much time will it take?
- Who else should be involved?
- What research must be done?
- What's the budget and timeline?

Brainstorming and mind mapping can help you answer these issues. From this you determine what activities, especially research, have to be done.

Your time and resources

- What will this proposal cost you in:
  - salaries and fees?
  - equipment and supplies?
  - travel?
- Can your cash flow handle it?

Establish deadlines and responsibilities

- What has to be done:
  - by when?
  - by whom?
- Priorities?
- Schedule it; e.g.,
  - surveys completed (date)
  - first draft (date)
  - final draft (date)

Budgeting your time and resources

How much money and time are you willing to spend on developing your proposal? Typical questions include:

- Will you have to pay extra staff and/or consultants?
- Are travel costs involved?
- What are the costs for presentation, equipment rental, research, writing and printing?
- Will this proposal cause problems with other work?
- Can your cash flow handle the added expenses?

These are the kinds of questions you must ask yourself and incorporate into your budget model.

What are the deadlines and responsibilities?

Proposals are almost always deadline driven. Sometimes the deadline is extended—you can certainly request it. It's more likely that missed deadlines will eliminate your bid.

It's therefore very important to come up with a critical path:

- What has to be done by when?
- Who does it?
- What are the priorities?
- What is the impact on other activities?

For example, you might include information such as:

- Surveys completed by (date)
- Research analysis completed by (date)
- First draft by (date)
- Final draft by (date)

If you can, give yourself space between completion and the submission date. Then, if anything comes up at the last minute—new information, corrections, adjustments—changes can be made.

Be flexible

Proposals require discipline, commitment and a willingness to work late to get the job done.

Flexibility

Proposals have a habit of turning into late nights and overtime. They require flexibility and commitment.

What if a client needs a proposal tomorrow? I recommend that you still do a quick plan on how you're going to proceed, based on that timeline.

Be careful on what you agree to. Better to give a preliminary report, or decline the proposal altogether, than make promises you can't keep.

Next steps

Your post-briefing session determines the steps to take for the proposal to get under way. The next section deals with the research you may need to do in order to develop a successful proposal.

The information you need

- About the proposal itself
- About the client
- About the client's industry and market

Landscape Scenario: **Information required**

Client:

- Previous housing development landscaping
- Commitment to ecology
- Short-term vs. long-term thinking

Residents:

- Survey preferences and concerns

Regulatory (government agencies):

- Environment
- Infrastructure/public safety

Site:

- Full inventory
- Keep or change/remove
- Low maintenance factors

Industry:

- Trends in landscape planning

III - RESEARCH

You have received considerable information from the client. Together with your team you formulate a plan on how to proceed with any research. There is no right order in doing research. Much of it may already have been done in preparation for the briefing or in assessing the RFP or proposal package. There are two basic questions:

1. What information do you need?
2. Where do you find it?

What information do you need?

The areas for which you may need information include:

- The proposal itself
- The client's organization
- The state of the client's industry

The proposal itself

What do you need to find out about the proposal request? For the Landscape Scenario, research concerns would include the site itself, the climate, residents' viewpoints, concerns of other stakeholders.

The client's organization

What are its mission and vision, goals and objectives?

What are its successes and challenges?

Who can you talk to? CEO, management, employees?

What do others say about it? Customers, media, competition, suppliers?

The state of the client's industry

How is this industry faring? Is it doing well? Is it in trouble? What is the impact of the economy?

Your job is to determine what information you need in the above, and/or other areas, to help you develop your proposal.

Finding the information

Your sources

- Primary (first-hand)
- Secondary (second-hand)

Landscape Scenario

Primary sources

- Full site survey, what's there now and the type of terrain
- Interviews with client staff
- Surveys of residents
- Interviews with regulators—planning departments, environment
- Land use impact studies
- Your own thinking and ideas

Secondary sources

- Industry magazines for current practices and standards
- Suppliers for "hardware," such as fences, playground equipment, lighting, ponds
- Internet—for any new research that might help this proposal

Where do you find the information?

Information comes from a variety of sources. Some of it is first-hand (**primary** sources), some second-hand (**secondary** sources).

Primary sources

The proposal package and briefing are always launch points. In the case of the Landscape Scenario, primary sources might include:

- Guided walk through the site
- Topographical maps
- Soil reports
- Residents' surveys
- Your own thoughts, ideas and experience

In discussing a client, primary sources might include:

- People directly connected with the organization - CEO, board of directors, staff and employees
- Customers, suppliers
- Corporate reporting such as:
  - annual reports
  - customer satisfaction surveys
  - market analysis
  - employee surveys
  - investment analysis
  - any surveys or reports that deal directly with the organization as well as statistical and financial information it generates

Secondary sources

- News reports
- Industry trade groups - e.g., statistical information on that industry or sector
- Comments from third parties, such as investment analysts
- Libraries (Periodicals/reports/CD-ROM databases)
- Internet and corporate Intranets
- Government documents

TALK TO THE RIGHT PEOPLE

- Decision makers
- Anyone who can make a valuable contribution
- Meet in person
- Be prepared

Specific research requirements

What we've listed under **primary** and **secondary** sources are the ***general*** places to look for information. What you must do is ***be specific*** in your research:

- Talk to the right people
- Speak with experts
- Consider the competition
- Check the regulators
- Use the Internet
- Corporate Intranets
- Other secondary sources

Talk to the right people

I'm going to belabor this point. Speak with the decision makers and anyone else who can shed a light on or make an important contribution to your research efforts. Too often people speak to appointees who may have inaccurate information or are way behind the decision timeline.

To get to the right people you often have to be very persistent. Those best qualified to help are usually the busiest. You may have to meet them for breakfast, or phone them at specific times. I prefer to meet in person because:

- You usually get far more information
- You get clarity
- Their responses often generate:
  - other questions
  - fresh and often unexpected perspectives
  - different approaches
- You build relationships

Be well prepared with the questions for which you want answers. If possible, supply your interviewees beforehand with your questions so they are better prepared and everyone's time is used more productively.

By speaking to the right people, you also gain a broader perspective on the proposal and why it is being requested. You may discover that the proposal actually deals with a different issue and has been requested in order to avoid looking at a troublesome situation. If that's the case, it may be smart to check back with the client to see if the proposal should continue.

Set interviews up early. The sooner these are completed, the better your grasp on what the client needs.

TALK TO EXPERTS

- Experts can get you:
  - key answers quickly
  - save you time
  - **but**, they may cost you

THE COMPETITION

- Client competitors:
  - state of client's marketplace
  - client's reputation in the industry
  - may discover if client is doing well or in trouble

Set up the interview as soon as possible! Get on the phone and contact people so you find out their views and what they need. If it involves the client, most clients will pave the way for you. However, make sure you get permission to do things that the client may be wary of. I was once involved in a proposal for a major courier company. They wanted to know how best to build a conference for their salespeople.

One approach was to find out what customers thought about the salespeople and build the conference around those findings. Behaviors customers didn't like could be addressed with training. Behaviors they applauded could be celebrated. The courier company, however, did not want us to check with their customers, even though it might have produced information to improve their customer service.

Talk to experts

It surprises me how willing experts can sometimes be to give you their time. Often, all you have to do is ask. For various reasons it can be hard to take that step. Fear is part of it. Another consideration is that experts don't have the time. That's an assumption. Talking to knowledgeable people, however, is a proactive step. I suggest you try it!

Consider the competition

Competitors are sources of information that may be very valuable. Specifically:

- The client's competition
- The other vendors

The client's competition. What kind of competitive market is your client involved in? How might this market, and the companies who compete in it, impact the client? What do you need to know about these competitors and the marketplace that will enhance or impact the way in which you draw up your proposal?

THE COMPETITION (cont'd)

- If you know the other vendors:
  - stress the benefits of using your company
  - if the project attracts multiple vendors, stay away unless you are convinced you can win

THE REGULATORS

- What impact might they have?

USE THE INTERNET

- #1 source of secondary information
- Cautionary tales:
  - be focused
  - narrow your search
  - is information valid and current?

CORPORATE INTRANETS

- Is client Intranet available?

OTHER SECONDARY SOURCES

- Newspapers, magazines
- Librarians

The other vendors. When you're in a specialized field, you often know who the other vendors are. If you do, stress the features and benefits of using your organization. At the same time, do not put down your competitors.

If there are many other vendors, you may decide that it's simply too competitive to submit a proposal. The same is true if you find that one competitor has close contacts to the client and is therefore the odds on favorite. It's far better to look for other opportunities unless you are convinced that you have a real chance of winning.

Check the regulators

Government regulations might have an impact on your proposal. For example, regulations that forbid smoking in restaurants or public places could influence any proposal you make in designing or marketing a restaurant.

How can the Internet help you?

The Internet has become the #1 source of secondary information for many of us. If you can't find answers elsewhere, there's probably a source on the Internet that will tell you. A few pieces of advice:

1. Narrow your search to find what you really need
2. Stay focused on your objectives
3. The sources you find on the Internet may be inaccurate and/or out of date. Check your sources carefully for accuracy

Corporate Intranets

Many companies have developed their own internal information system—an Intranet. If available, the Intranet may produce information of value to your proposal.

Other secondary sources

Newspapers and magazines are often good sources, especially for information about the economy and its various sectors. Qualified librarians can also be very helpful, not only in finding information, but pointing you in the right direction.

Record the information

- What it is
- Where it comes from
- Who was responsible for it
- Access date

Research analysis

- What have we got?
- What does it tell us?

Brainstorm or mind map your findings for effective analysis.

Record the information

Where did you find the information and how will you record it? Depending on the volume of information you've collected, you may choose to use a computer database, flip charts, index cards, files and filing cabinets.

Make sure, in recording the information, that you write down what the information was about, where it came from and the date. For example:

- Interview with Susan Hepworth, VP Human Resources, on changes in company pension plans. March 18, 2004.

Should you feel it necessary to include these sources in your proposal, you can do it informally as a series of notes, like the one above. Or you could use formal reference systems such as the Modern Language Association (MLA) or the American Psychological Association (APA). In the Appendix we show you how to reference your material using MLA and APA guidelines.

RESEARCH ANALYSIS

The questions to ask yourself once you've done your research are:

- What have we found out?
- What does it mean?

It's a smart idea to brainstorm the information that comes out of your research. Include everyone's input, get the ideas down and examine what you've got.

The results may confirm what you already know and the approaches you've been considering for the proposal. They might indicate that you should simply tweak your approach in order to come up with a solid solution.

Sometimes the results create totally new options that are outside your previously suggested solutions. Sometimes the results leave you less certain of one approach, and you start to look at others.

What if results indicate that:

a. The proposal is not valid?

b. Changes should be made?

Let the client decide how to proceed.

Landscape Scenario: **Initial research findings**

A small, sample survey of Glen Arran Estates residents indicates that they want good play areas, open space and an emphasis on safety.

We talked with regulators about the wetlands and they insist that the area be maintained. They may be open to negotiation on how this is to be done.

The client's own staff have told us that maintenance is a sensitive issue. In two recent projects, the plan for recreation areas turned out to be more expensive than originally estimated, particularly annual maintenance. Keeping maintenance costs under control must be a high priority.

What if the results appear negative?

Your results may also lead you to question whether the proposal should go ahead. If this happens, it's appropriate to discuss the situation with the client and get a firm answer. Should it still go ahead, or be modified in some way or even be dropped? The last thing you want is to continue working on a proposal with an uncertain future.

My wife was once involved in a proposal to develop a promotional video for a new senior citizens' residence and care facility. The owners wanted to show the video to seniors to encourage them to purchase the units. Shortly after touring the facility, we discovered that the units were selling out faster than management had anticipated. Recognizing that the video was not required, we informed the client and the project was shelved.

Next steps

Sound research and analysis give you a solid foundation on which to proceed to the next step—developing a proposal that will best answer the needs of the client.

Why should the client select you?

Because your Unique Selling Proposition (USP) will best execute the proposal

What is your USP?

- Reputation?
- Experience?
- Innovation?
- Work already done for this client?
- Price?
- People?
- Brilliant idea?
- Ability to execute?

All of these, alone, or in combination, can set your proposal apart.

IV - USP: YOUR UNIQUE SELLING PROPOSITION

The research is complete—now it's time to come up with the key element to your proposal. What makes you and your proposal new, better and different and the one to best serve the client? It could be an idea, a new product, a new service, a good price. It could be as simple as your particular skills. You put out oil fires better than anyone else. You may charge more but time is critical.

If you can come up with a better idea, a better mousetrap, a new and innovative way to do something, or do it more economically, or faster, or whatever the criteria happen to be, you are likely to get the job.

So what makes you or your organization unique or different? It is your Unique Selling Proposition or USP.

USP: Your Unique Selling Proposition

You know what your unique characteristics are as you prepare your approach to the proposal. They might include:

- Your reputation as an expert in your field
- Your experience
- Your ability to innovate
- Work you've already done for this client
- Price—you may be the lowest bidder
- The people you gather for your team
- The brilliant idea that sets you apart from competitors
- Your ability to execute and follow through

The right USP will drive the whole presentation. What you do is tailor your USP to the challenges of the proposal. So the USP might be a combination of a number of things—such as your ability to put together a great team and execute an approach that appeals to the client.

The right USP

Tailor your USP to the proposal. Influencing factors are:

- Clarity on client's present situation and where they want to go
- What the research tells you
- Exploration of all possibilities

Some USPs are obvious. Others may require diligence and dedication to come up with the right idea.

Stand out from the competition

Give added value

- Make this proposal special
- Could your other experiences benefit this client?
- Could your approach benefit the client in another area, beyond the scope of the proposal?

Coming up with the right USP

I have been involved in many proposals. I've seen people struggle to come up with what they believe is the right approach. Lots of ideas get tossed around, examined and discarded. Sometimes the USP is obvious or comes very quickly. Other times a dedicated team has to explore several options. A number of things help you decide:

- Absolute clarity on where the client is now and where they want to go
- Taking a close look at what the research tells you
- Getting together with your team and examining all the possibilities raised by your collective input

Stand out from the competition

Three things can contribute to your ability to stand out:

- Give added value
- Involve the team
- Encourage risk taking

Give added value

What features and benefits will have you stand out or differentiate you from the competition? How will you give this client added value? Even if you're the logical choice due to your expertise, look for ways to make this proposal special, perhaps a way to execute it that you've not tried before. Whatever it is, always look for ways to excel:

- What is so compelling in your approach that it grabs the attention of the client?
- What difference has your experience/expertise made to other clients? What ideas of yours have benefited them? Might they apply here? Is there cross fertilization?
- Are there other benefits to the client beyond the scope of the proposal itself? Sometimes a client may have other objectives that your approach will accomplish. Is this something the client would like to know about?

Involve the team

- Diversity works
- Everyone is encouraged to participate—staff, outside consultants, even suppliers
- Committed teams can be a good fit to work with the client's own team

Involve the team

The team has the potential to make you and your organization the winner. Team members bring:

- Their own expertise to the table
- A whole host of suggestions that can make all the difference between winning and being runner up
- The potential that lies in working together
- A commitment to work with the client's own team

A team's value lies in its diversity. It can usually come up with a variety of approaches—ways to scale, get around or go through walls, or check whether a wall is an obstacle in the first place and should simply be avoided.

I was once involved with a major proposal for the launch of a new truck in a large convention center. We had a great team of people working on the project. The big question was—how do you best reveal this new truck to the audience? Visually, we wanted a startling revelation, preferably having the truck come through a paper screen decorated with the corporate logo.

Convention center regulations forbade starting the engine while the show was on. Since we could not drive the truck forward, we opted to reveal the new vehicle with an elaborate screen opening accompanied by appropriate music and indoor fireworks. It would have been very effective.

We didn't win. One of the competitors had a better idea. They built a ramp and prior to the show, backed the vehicle up onto it. When it came time to reveal the truck, a driver simply released the brakes. The truck rolled forward, its momentum enough to break through the screen and create the desired effect.

It's that kind of thinking that produces winning proposals.

Encourage risk taking

- Align the team to work together to develop the best solution
- Urge people to take risks and put unconventional ideas on the table

It may be easy to come up with the right USP. It may also take a long, tough and dedicated team effort.

Landscape Scenario: **Your USP**

As a landscape architect, your USP is your unique four quadrant design strategy incorporating four key elements:

- Economic to create and maintain
- Pertinent to the local ecology
- A place people love to be in
- Usable in all four seasons

The four quadrant design strategy is innovative and extremely flexible. This strategy is enhanced by your company's reputation for:

- A commitment to work with the client and other stakeholders
- The remarkable team you bring together to achieve the deliverables

Encourage risk taking

Sometimes we're afraid to take risks, concerned about what others may think. And yet that is what will often set one proposal apart from another—the willingness to take a risk and come up with something unique that works for the client.

In order for this to happen, there has to be a climate where risks are possible—where anyone on the team, or any outside advisors, are encouraged to come up with ideas and make suggestions, regardless of how outlandish their ideas and suggestions appear to be. The best ideas, the best USPs, show up when everyone feels that their contribution is important and makes a difference.

The value of using exploration tools, such as brainstorming and mind mapping, emphasized throughout this book, is that they help to get those who are risk averse to make important contributions.

Bottom line

You want every idea on the table. For these ideas to be of value, certain factors must be in place:

- Everyone clearly understands the client's current position
- Everyone clearly understands where the client wants to go and the obstacles or walls that may be in the way
- Everyone is aligned with finding the solution
- Everyone works together to produce the result

Implementing your solution

The client needs to:

- Appreciate what you intend to do
- Be confident that you can pull it off

Provide a critical path:

- Phase 1
  - objectives
  - tasks
  - deliverables (results)
  - by when
- Phase 2
  - objectives
  - tasks
  - deliverables (results)
  - by when
- Phase 3 etc.

IMPLEMENTING YOUR SOLUTION

Preamble

The client needs to know how you plan to execute your proposal so that they are confident that you can do the job.

Most proposals with which I've been involved have required considerable creativity. Several other organizations are competing against us. The client is going to receive a number of ideas to resolve a particular issue.

Most of the time you can be confident that the client will respect your ideas and solutions and act with integrity.

However, on rare occasions, if a client sees a particularly interesting idea, they may decide that they can do it themselves and dismiss all vendors. Or they may like part of one proposal and part of another, give the project to one of the bidders, but ask them to incorporate this other idea.

You have to assess just how much information to provide so that the client is confident that yours is the best approach, and that you are best equipped to implement it.

Implementation—critical path

Any proposal, large or small, requires some kind of implementation plan. Obviously that's more complex for a major sales meeting than providing a quotation for some lumber and delivering it to a local construction site. Both, however, need ***a critical path***.

This path or plan establishes the phases for completing the proposal, the objectives of each phase, the tasks required to complete the objectives, and the results (deliverables).

Phases

Splitting a proposal into phases allows a proposal to be completed step by step. Both client and vendor can evaluate the status of the project at any time, thus ensuring orderly progress.

Landscape Scenario: **USP implementation**

- Develop unique four quadrant design strategy
- Emphasize flexible use with minimal maintenance
- Meet high aesthetic and environmental standards
- Allow for full four season use
- Survey Glen Arran Estates residents on park features
- Conduct in depth site survey, working with the developer, and determine general work to be done
- Focus on environmental and flooding concerns in SE section
- Prepare preliminary playground needs with graded levels of equipment from toddler through elementary
- Consider play slopes for summer and winter use
- Do preliminary make up of appropriate trees, shrubs

Split project into three phases:

Phase 1 (Jan. 30)

Objective - complete site survey; carry out and analyze results of residents' survey

Tasks - total site survey with client (includes guided tour)
- pay special attention to flood issues
- carry out survey of residents

Deliverables - inventory of site
- analysis of flooding issues
- residents' survey results

Phase 2 (Feb. 20)

Objective - present preliminary plans

Tasks - work with site information, residents' views and regulatory information, and assess physical needs; e.g., soil, pathways

Deliverables - present plan to client and residents for input

Phase 3 (Mar. 19)

Objective - deliver final four quadrant design strategy

Tasks - develop final plans from stakeholder input
- provide client with potential contractor construction schedule

Deliverables - give client final plan, providing various cost options

Establishing strategic messages to stakeholders

The objectives for each phase are set out in strategic messages to key audiences. These messages deliver the rationale for the tasks required by each phase and the deliverables. As well, **completion dates** are attached to all aspects of these phases. Using the Landscape Scenario as an example, there are three phases:

Phase 1 - Complete site inventory and analysis of residents' survey

Phase 2 - Present preliminary plans for the site

Phase 3 - Deliver four quadrant design strategy

The key Phase I message to both client and resident is:

We must have a solid foundation on which to base this landscaping development. That requires full, physical knowledge of the site plus feedback from residents (the users) on what they want to see.

Therefore the tasks are:

- Extensive site survey to determine inventory
- Residents' survey—preparation, client approval, take survey and analyze the results

The intended deliverables are:

- Detailed site plan—all facets of the site, its problems and challenges have been identified
- Residents' survey results—we know what residents want to see on the site

All proposals need this kind of work plan for implementation, detailing the objectives, how the objectives will be achieved (tasks) and what the intended results are (the deliverables). This plan becomes the basis for implementing your USP.

Next steps

You have developed your USP—your Unique Selling Proposition—and how you will implement the proposal request. Now you need to put the proposal together.

Proposal format

- Letter of transmittal/ Cover letter
- Title page
- Executive summary
- Table of contents
- Detailed explanation of proposal
- Background information and logistics
- Appendix

Landscape Scenario: **Cover letter**

December 22, 2003

Alan Sigurdson
General Manager
Western Associates

Dear Mr. Sigurdson:

Re: Glen Arran Estates Landscape Plan

We are pleased to present our proposal for providing an architectural landscape design for Glen Arran Estates as per your request of December 12, 2003.

Our four quadrant design strategy will meet the needs of not only a responsible developer, but also the residents of Glen Arran Estates. We are confident that our team, whose skills and talents have given our firm an outstanding reputation in this field, will work well with your people to serve the needs of all stakeholders.

We believe that this project, if begun by January 10, would allow site construction to begin this spring...

V - WRITING UP THE PROPOSAL

Format

Parts I through IV explain the process of developing a proposal. Part V puts the proposal together in writing. A number of format elements make up the proposal. Not all elements are necessary, depending on the size, scope and formality of the proposal. You may want to check with the client to see what elements they'd like to see. However, here is a general format to follow:

1. Letter of transmittal/Cover letter
2. Title page
3. Executive summary
4. Table of contents
5. Detailed explanation of the proposal
   - introduction to the situation
   - research and analysis
   - your solution and its implementation
6. Background information
   - your company/organization
   - your people
7. Logistics
   - budget
   - roles and responsibilities
8. Appendix

Make all areas equally strong

If one area is weaker than another, evaluators or the client may simply rule you out of the running, never looking at your great idea to solve their problem. So make sure you have spent sufficient time on all areas of the RFP/proposal request, not just those you consider most important.

Letter of transmittal/Cover letter

A letter of transmittal goes at the front of a formal proposal, addressed to the person who authorized the RFP/proposal. The letter refers to the request, summarizes key parts and indicates what the next steps are. A cover letter is similar though it may be a little less formal, and attached to the proposal or form part of it. These letters may even take the place of an executive summary.

Executive summary

- Summary of proposal (in more depth than letter of transmittal)

Landscape Scenario: **Executive summary**

Glen Arran Estates is a planned single family development close to the country yet within easy transit to the city core...a place for young families to grow and share their neighborhood...

As a responsible developer, Western Associates wishes to see landscaping that matches their commitment to distinctive housing, but very importantly retains low maintenance costs.

Research indicates residents' desire for a four seasons park, concern from environment officials about preserving wetlands, and the need for substantial resources to bring the park up to acceptable standards.

Our planned four quadrant design strategy will reconfigure the current site into four season usage...

We have assembled a team whose talents have transformed similar areas in new communities. If started by January 10, this project can be completed in time for spring site construction...

Introduction to the situation

- Convince the client that you understand their situation and their objectives

Landscape Scenario: **Introduction to situation**

As developer of Glen Arran Estates, Western Associates requires landscaping to meet the high standards set by the construction of the homes. As well, homeowners must feel that this park is very much a central part of their community, along with stores, schools and other facilities. In particular, it must meet the needs of Glen Arran Estates' key demographic—young families...

The objective is to transform the existing terrain into a warm and inviting four seasons park where families can play, relax and feel as if it is an extension of their neighborhood. At the same time, the proposed solution must meet budget requirements for capital, and more especially, ongoing maintenance costs...

If you're a supplier responding to a proposal request to you alone, or you've submitted a speculative proposal, you can put in it a place for the client to sign, authorizing you to proceed with the proposal. The letter must contain a clear offer and a clear acceptance. The client will retain a copy and return the signed copy to you. It will then be a legal contract.

Title page

The title page contains the name of the proposal (if RFP include any title or number), client's name, date, name of supplier. It can sometimes include the author's name.

Executive summary

This section summarizes what your proposal is about, highlighting key points:

- It explains the present situation so the client is clear that you understand it, emphasizing any challenges the client is facing
- It explains what the client desires to have happen
- It summarizes any research and analysis and identifies major findings and conclusions
- It lays out your solution, why this solution will resolve any negative situation or bring about a satisfying result. It describes how the solution will be implemented
- It summarizes budget and timelines
- It states what has to happen for the proposal to proceed

Some proposals, rather than using an executive summary, make up a ***Highlights*** page designed to reflect the key points.

DETAILED EXPLANATION OF THE PROPOSAL

Introduction to the situation and desired result

This introductory section must confirm that you understand, from the client's point of view:

- What the current situation is
- What the client wants to achieve
- Any issues or concerns the client has in achieving the desired result

Research and analysis

- Details the research you did
- Your conclusions

Landscape Scenario: **Research findings**

We carried out research in four main areas:

1. A brief survey of Glen Arran Estates residents. We found that residents really wanted a safe, attractive park close by, where they could play with their children...
2. Two interviews with Western Associates management. We found that the company had major concerns in other projects because of the high cost of park maintenance...
3. A preliminary inventory of the area...and what would be required in any proposal to bring it to standard and prevent flooding in the southeast section of the site.
4. We checked with environmental regulators. Their main requirement was to retain wetlands in the southeast section.

Your USP

How you are going to resolve the client's issue, situation or need...

Landscape Scenario: **USP**

We propose a four quadrant design strategy to the landscaping issues at Glen Arran Estates. This approach, applied successfully elsewhere, focuses on creating a four seasons park, a place people love coming to, that's ecologically sound and economical to run. Incorporated into this planning are both the requests of residents and your concerns as client.

...and how you will implement it

Phase 1 - Total site survey and residents' survey (Jan. 30)

Phase 2 - Preliminary plans, based on site survey and residents' survey, and consultation with regulatory authorities (Feb. 20)

Phase 3 - Detail plans, ready for bid by contractor (Mar. 19)

If you can also add value by providing additional information or knowledge that adds to the client's own understanding, you may well boost your chances of success. This section should clearly convey to the client "This supplier understands our problem, or situation, as well as we do. They appreciate what we want to achieve."

Research and analysis

This section provides sufficient details of the research you've undertaken, why you did it, and the results. You stress what part the research played in identifying the best course of action to achieve the client's objectives.

Sometimes research becomes part of the proposal itself. In one situation, the company I was working with advised the client not to proceed with major restructuring without first surveying senior management attitudes. In accepting our proposal, the client agreed that such a survey was critical as restructuring would involve senior managers responsible for implementing difficult changes.

Your solution - your USP

You tell the client how you are going to resolve the problem or situation. This can be a very short description if it's simply a quotation for a product you manufacture, or more elaborate if the proposal entails planning a major conference with an awards ceremony.

You focus on your USP—whether it be your specific experience, background or skill sets; your expertise in designing a building or creativity in producing a music video; or simply your ability to supply a product or service at the right price.

You also convey, in broad strokes, how you will implement your solution. As well, you provide the client with a critical path indicating what the phases (if any) are, their objectives, the tasks required to achieve those objectives, and the results or deliverables.

Background information

Highlighting your ability to do the job

Your company/organization

- Who you are
- Your experience
- Your commitments
- Unique factors
- Endorsements

Your people

- Names/qualifications
- Unique factors applicable to this project
- Strengths
- Outsourced experts

BACKGROUND INFORMATION

Why choose you?

The client needs to know about the competence of:

- Your company/organization
- Your people

This information has one primary objective: to highlight your ability to do the job. This is particularly important if you're new to the client and even to the business. You may have a brilliant solution to their problems, but you've only been in operation for six months. Your competitor has been a client supplier for over a decade. What credibility do you have to do the job? A secondary, yet in many ways no less important factor, is building a partnership with the client.

Your company/organization

A brief account of your organization, its achievements and objectives. Background information includes:

- Your qualifications and experience
- The kind of business you have carried on, where and for how long
- Projects you have carried out, especially those similar to the present proposal and the results you achieved
- Endorsements from third parties, especially satisfied clients, plus any articles written or awards received
- A list of clients (often provided only on request)
- References (usually provided only on request)

Your people

This part names:

- Key people who will be involved in carrying out the proposal, their qualifications and their roles
- Other major resources; e.g., if you're doing a sales video, add the names of post production companies and musicians whose work is important to the project

Logistics

Budget

- Based on scope of project
- Line item or lump sum?
- Contingencies
- Conditions
- Options
- Delays

Payment terms

- Depends on project:
  - straight invoice
  - series of payments
    e.g., 1/3, 1/3, 1/3
    e.g., based on degree of completion

Sign off at the completion of each stage

LOGISTICS

Budget

Depending on the industry, budgets are either broken down by line item or acceptable as a lump sum. RFPs/RFQs for equipment and supplies may be acceptable as a lump sum. RFPs for projects and services usually require bidders to break down their budget into cost areas.

Clients with informal proposals either request or appreciate cost breakdowns. What a cost breakdown may do is allow the client to decide whether they want a particular part of a proposal or not. For example, if the client is planning a sales meeting, but does not require staging as listed in the budget, staging can be taken out.

As the supplier, make sure you build in a fair return plus an allowance for contingencies—usually 5-10%, depending on the project and the budget.

Options

RFPs don't usually include options. In other proposals, it is perfectly acceptable to provide options, unless specifically requested not to or the budget is fixed. A client will often come to you, detail a situation, and ask what you can do for a budget of $25,000. Your response might be something like—for $25,000 we can complete Phase 1 by June 27. For an additional $10,000 we can complete Phase 2 by July 31.

Delays

If special conditions cause you to incur added costs, such as delays due to strikes or weather or anything beyond your control, these costs should be above and beyond the approved budget.

Payment terms

If not already established under the terms of the RFP or proposal package, set out the terms you expect. Projects are often paid on a percentage of completion basis; e.g., building contracts. It could also be three equal payments, each 1/3 of the total contract, to be paid at specific stages.

Signing off at each stage

Part of the agreement with the client is that the client must sign off after each stage of the project is completed. Once sign off occurs, any further changes are not part of the existing budget and are subject to extra billing.

Roles and responsibilities

- Defined in RFP
- Informal proposal may be more flexible and open to discussion in areas such as:
  - what you will do
  - what the client will do
  - logistics
  - timelines
  - levels of cooperation

Appendix

Details additional information useful to the client but not required in body of proposal

Roles and responsibilities

With RFPs, the roles and responsibilities of the client and the supplier are set out in the document and take effect at the awarding of the contract. With other proposals they may also be clearly identified. If not, it may be appropriate to lay out roles and responsibilities, particularly if the client and the supplier need to partner on certain "executional" elements of the project in order to realize maximum resource and cost efficiencies. In this type of scenario, the proposal should clearly include:

- How the project is going to be completed and implemented; i.e. client and supplier responsibilities for "executional" elements
- The logistics involved; e.g., planning meetings, etc.
- Timelines for the project
- Others who might be involved
- What cooperation is required not only from the client, but perhaps from client customers and suppliers

APPENDIX

An appendix is a place to put any additional information which you believe might be useful for the client to know, but is not necessary in the main body of the proposal; e.g., annual reports, bulletins, drawings.

Make sure you thoroughly read your proposal

- Read it out loud:
  - does it flow?
  - anything missing?
  - anything unnecessary?

- Have a disinterested party familiar with the topic read your proposal and get their comments or suggestions

Design

- Support your words with:
  - graphics
  - pictures
  - charts

CAVEAT:

A picture may be worth a thousand words...provided that there is excellence of content.

VI - OTHER CONSIDERATIONS

You know what your proposal is about—you've done the research and come up your approach. You've dealt with budget and responsibilities. Here are some final, but important things to consider:

- Read your proposal
- Design of the proposal
- Presenting the proposal
- Importance of follow up
- Post mortem if you don't get the project
- Last minute tips

Read your proposal

I suggest taking the following actions:

a. Read the proposal out loud. Is it clear? Is it accurate? Does it make sense? Does it flow? Is anything missing? Is anything superfluous? Does the tone and manner of the writing convey what you wish to convey? As well, reading out loud means that you are more likely to catch incorrect spelling, poor grammar and other factors important to the credibility of the proposal.

b. Have someone else read it, preferably someone with no interest in the proposal other than to assist you, yet familiar enough with the topic to comment on whether it works, raise new issues and suggest changes.

Design of the proposal

Publishing and presentation software can make today's proposals look very professional. In particular, a proposal can be visually broken up with words, charts and illustrations. These can all make a difference in getting your message to the client both powerfully and effectively.

I make one caveat. Don't let appearance take precedence over content. There's sometimes a tendency to dazzle the client with glitz to gloss over deficiencies in content. A professional presentation by one individual, with minimal or even no audiovisual support, can sometimes have as much or more impact than a whole lot of glitz.

Presenting the proposal

- Provides a flavor of your approach:
  - personal and flexible
  - opportunity for creative delivery
  - allows client to ask questions
  - allows you to clarify points as well as clear up objections and misunderstandings
  - helps build relationship

Do not simply read your proposal to the client.

Make sure you follow up!

Presenting the proposal

A client may make a decision based on a written proposal alone. This is more likely if the proposal is small, the budget low or the proposal fairly straightforward.

In more complex projects, the client may ask half a dozen companies to bid, stating that the three top bidders will be short-listed and asked to make a presentation in person.

I prefer to present in person, with team members. It gives the client the opportunity to ask questions and raise objections. This allows your team both to answer the objections and to expand on your approach. (Ask yourself what questions the client is likely to ask and be well prepared with answers.) It helps build relationship, credibility and trust.

In making your presentation, what the client wants is a flavor of what you're proposing. Innovative ways to present are usually welcomed. They send a signal to the client about your organization and your willingness to take risks.

A colleague once submitted a proposal to an organization concerned with the high costs of automobile insurance. The presentation was done down a hallway, with a long sheet of paper carefully unrolled as a highway. As they came to highway signs and intersections, each step in solving the client's problems was carefully explained, using traffic terminology. They won the contract.

The importance of follow up

It's a simple rule. If you're not going to follow up, don't bother to write the proposal. I cannot stress this enough. Too many people lose proposals, sales and opportunities because they fail to follow up.

Okay! So the client tells you that they will let you know within a certain period of time. In most cases, that happens. But this isn't a perfect world. In many other cases, you're kept waiting...and waiting. You assume that the proposal's been awarded to someone else. That may be true and the client, for some reason, has failed to contact you.

Clients do not always inform bidders by the specified time

- They may have told the winner but not other bidders
- Made no contact because:
  - priorities have changed
  - personnel problem
  - proposal no longer necessary
  - external circumstances—weather, market conditions

Be proactive and call. You may find other opportunities.

Post mortem

Why didn't you get the job?

FIND OUT! Ask the client.

- Prepare questions for which you want answers
- Don't be confrontational
- Acquire valuable input for future bids

It's also possible that something else has happened:

- The customer's priorities have changed—perhaps because of financial issues or labor problems that you would not be aware of
- A personnel problem—the person you were dealing with is sick, left, or had to work on another assignment
- A decision has been made that the proposal is no longer necessary or should be delayed
- External circumstances—weather, transportation, markets—any of these might delay a decision

The point is, you don't know. Until you do, you're operating under assumptions. Assume nothing. Follow up. Maybe the decision's been delayed. Maybe they're going to award you the contract but wanted to wait until the CEO had returned from vacation.

You may also find out that the client found no proposal acceptable—or that they liked some of your proposal and some from another vendor and weren't sure how to proceed. If the proposal wasn't quite what the customer wanted, you may get an opportunity to discuss it and come back with an alternative.

Here's another possibility. If the client likes you and your approach, they may be willing to work with you to come up with a proposal that does work for them.

So, if you haven't heard by a certain date, call. The worst that can happen is that you didn't win. More likely, no decision has been made or there are other reasons you were not aware of.

Post mortem *if* you don't get it

It can be very useful to find out why you did not get the job. Clients are often willing to explain why, which gives you the opportunity to learn so that you can be aware of any shortcomings next time. Here are a couple of things to bear in mind:

- Prepare the questions to which you want answers; e.g., Did you cover the mandatory requirements? If not, where did you fall short?
- Don't be confrontational. The objective is to learn so that you can do a better job next time

Last minute tips

- Don't play it safe
- Focus on the objective
- Remember the KISS principle—"Keep it simple"
- Make sure the proposal flows
- Be considerate to the evaluators or reviewers—they might reciprocate!

Last minute tips

Here is some last minute advice. We've made these points in other places throughout this book. However this may be a timely reminder.

- ***Don't play it safe***! Many customers want innovative thinking and better ways to solve their problems. That's why they come to you. If you can deliver just a bit more, a little extra, you may have the edge in winning the proposal.
- ***Stay focused on the main objective***. Don't lose sight of where you're going. It's easy to get sidetracked. Keep that objective in focus at all times.
- ***The KISS principle***. Where you can, keep your proposal as clean, elegant and simple as possible. And even if it's complex, keep the descriptive easy to follow. Time is the critical factor. If your proposal is the right idea or approach, succinctly told, your client will be very appreciative. This also means avoiding superfluous comments as well as adjectives to embellish your writing.
- ***Look for flow***. Your proposal should flow from start to finish, each section logically following from the previous one and leading to the next. Check by reading the proposal out loud.
- ***Help evaluators/reviewers***. Remember that evaluators or reviewers have other proposals to go through. Make yours easy for them to follow, shorter rather than longer, and where appropriate use bullets to make your points. And only provide what they need to know. (Any additional information can be added into an appendix).

Sales Letters

A sales letter is a letter designed so effectively that it:

- Encourages a customer to buy your product or service
- Persuades a customer to give to a cause that you are promoting
- Provides an opportunity for you to meet a potential client face to face and begin building a business relationship

A sales letter may be:

- Initial contact for ongoing business
- Only contact
- Follow up contact

WHAT IS A SALES LETTER?

A sales letter has a number of purposes. A primary purpose is to encourage customers to buy your product or service. Its job is to first grab the customers' attention, then persuade them to take advantage of whatever product or service you have to offer.

Another purpose, particularly important to entrepreneurs and small businesses, is as an introduction to your organization. This allows you to get a face to face meeting with potential clients and build business relationships.

Who uses sales letters?

Organizations of all kinds, private and public, profit and nonprofit, use sales letters to market their particular products and services. Sales letters may be used in the start up of an organization to help get it off the ground. They may continue to be used to maintain sales over the years. Organizations that use sales letters extensively include magazine publishers, financial organizations, and charitable agencies of all kinds. Every day, these organizations send out thousands of letters in the form of direct mail, faxes and increasingly by e-mail.

In your research, you'll find that there are several sources of sample sales letters that can be adapted for your purposes, in books and via the Internet. It's important to understand, however, the rationale behind writing these letters so that you can always create something that works for your specific business.

Type of contact

A sales letter may be:

Your initial contact for ongoing business—this is your first contact with the customer. You may keep communicating by letter, or more likely by phone, fax, e-mail or in person.

Your only contact—the customer receives the letter, likes what he or she sees, and orders. You may send out 1000 letters. You may only get a response rate of 1-2%. For some businesses that's exactly what they expect. Any greater response is a bonus. All you do is fill the order.

Your follow up to an earlier contact—you may have spoken to the customer by phone or met at a trade fair or conference. The letter sets out what you have to offer, confirmation of terms and so on.

The content of the sales letter must:

- Demonstrate the need for your product or service
- Say why the customer should choose you
- Detail benefits
- Specify actions to be taken
- Provide an immediate incentive
- Establish relationship

Target audience

- *Specific individual/organization:*
  - personal letter
  - know name/title of contact
  - establish relationship to build business

- *Category based:*
  - target group; e.g., particular industry or professional organization
  - get name/title of decision maker

- *Widely based:*
  - very wide distribution; e.g., all households in a particular area
  - direct mail, mass faxes or e-mail

Content

Whether the sales letter is the initial introduction, only introduction, or a follow up to your offering, it must:

- Demonstrate the market's need for your product/service
- State why the customer should choose you, and if possible, your success in serving that industry sector
- Detail the benefits to the customer
- Specify what actions you and the customer might take
- Provide an incentive to act now—an offer they can't refuse
- Establish a favorable relationship, however brief

Targeting your audience

Sales letters can be targeted specifically, by category, or widely, based on the market you wish to reach.

Specific

A specific sales letter goes, wherever possible, to someone whose name and title you already know and preferably with whom you've been in contact. It can help create relationship and is therefore of value in building your business.

Category based

A category based sales letter might be one that is directed to a particular industry or group; e.g., construction companies, insurance companies, professional groups such as nurses and lawyers. If you know the name and title of the decision maker, so much the better. The letter then becomes more personal and gives you a higher chance of success.

Widely based

This sales letter goes to a much wider target market; e.g., to all households in a particular area, to a particular ethnic group, to an electorate by politicians. These are often direct mail, mass faxes or e-mail.

In this section on sales letters, the focus is on specific and category based sales letters.

Your sales letter competes with everything else your customer has to deal with—business and personal.

How will yours stand out so that the customer remembers you?

What you're up against

Your letter is competing with everything else clamoring for your customer's attention, such as other letters (competitors with products or services like yours), phone calls, faxes, e-mails, meetings, reports due, and all kinds of personal time demands.

Your objective is to have your letter achieve ***top of mind*** awareness where customers keep thinking about what you have to offer and act on it—now, next week, or a year from now.

Summary

So, what will make your letter so attractive, so compelling, so appealing that the customer does indeed decide to act?

There are three steps to writing that letter:

Step I - Establishing content and market

Step II - Determining format

Step III - Writing & revising

To examine the process, we've created a scenario about a small computer services company, Zephyr Computer Services. Zephyr plans to send out sales letters to potential clients, usually as a follow up to an initial phone contact.

Zephyr Scenario

Zephyr Computer Services was formed six months ago by five individual computer service specialists, each with extensive experience in the contracting industry.

Their prime target market is small- and medium-sized contracting firms, with a secondary market of small manufacturers.

What product or service are you offering the customer?

- Can you identify it?
- What promise about it can you deliver?

Zephyr Scenario: **Service to customers**

Zephyr provides its customers with:

- Service response if something goes wrong from 8 to 8 weekdays and 8 to noon Saturdays
- Technical excellence
- Education—we take the time to show you what happened and how to fix it so you may not need us next time

The promise? ***"We're as close as your phone with extended business hours. If you have a computer or systems problem, we'll fix it and get you back to work."***

I - ESTABLISHING CONTENT & MARKET

There are two questions that you must be able to answer in establishing key content for the sales letter. They are:

- What product or service do you offer?
- Who is your customer?

What product or service do you offer?

Too many organizations—profit/nonprofit—are unclear on what it is that their product and/or service actually offers the customer. I recommend that you use exploration tools (pages 36-47) to help you get clear. Then write out a statement, or promise on how your product/service will benefit the customer. This promise can be a powerful part of your letter. Check the following examples.

A national company has developed a new motor oil for the trucking industry specially formulated by type of engine. Customers who use it will benefit by:

a. Saving on maintenance and repairs
b. Improved gas mileage

The promise? Probably something like ***"Our oils keep your trucks on the road longer, and at lower cost."*** A fleet manager can identify with that.

Here's another example from a company that imported light fixtures for the office and retail sector. These fixtures provided exceptional lighting that looked great and lasted a long time, requiring only minimal maintenance and power.

The promise? ***"Our lighting superbly displays your product while consistently keeping your utilities and maintenance costs down."***

In the case of Zephyr Computer Services, their research has told them that customers want peace of mind—when something goes wrong, they want it to be fixed as soon as possible. They have therefore developed extended hours from 8-8 weekdays and from 8-noon on Saturdays. On the opposite page are some key elements for their sales letter.

Know your customer

This determines:

- Person/organization to whom your letter will go
- Appropriate style
- What attracts their interest

Zephyr Scenario: **Audience/style/interest**

The main audience is the small- to medium-sized contractor. This is the area the individual owners worked with prior to joining together. They see similar opportunities with small manufacturing businesses.

Zephyr will be contacting the companies first by phone to speak with key personnel to determine who should receive the letter and to begin to establish a relationship.

The style and tone will be conversational, addressing the frustrations that clients face when systems fail to work as expected.

The letter will make clear that Zephyr can solve their problems quickly, assuring their peace of mind.

Who is your customer?

Your customer is the organization or individual with the greatest likelihood of using your product or service. Determining that market, their wants, needs and desires is fundamental research. Knowing your customer determines:

- Where your letter will go
- The style most suited to that audience
- What will attract their interest

With the motor oil, you'd focus on companies with fleets of trucks to maintain, the customer being the fleet manager. With lighting systems your customer might be individual store/office owners or the maintenance managers of multiple store/office operations.

You now have to determine the style best suited to these two audiences. You can be fairly sure that it will be a warm, conversational tone. The attraction in both cases will be to the benefits of reducing costs and having a better product to serve their respective businesses—the right oil for the trucks, the right lighting for stores and offices.

With Zephyr Computer Services, the style will be conversational in tone, emphasizing the peace of mind that clients feel in knowing that, whenever possible, Zephyr's partners will fix any problems at a moment's notice.

Is your customer the consumer?

What if your business is dealing more with the consumer as customer rather than a business as customer? The tone and style of the letter to your consumer may reflect a friendly, conversational tone. On the other hand the style may exhibit extra ***enthusiasm*** for the product, with strong emphasis on features and benefits. For example, you may have a business that delivers frozen meat products direct to homeowners, with special discounts for bulk buys. Your sales letter will have a strong ***act now*** focus!

Next steps

The knowledge of your product/service and its benefits must now be crafted into a format that captures the customer's attention.

AIDA principle

Create:

- **A**ttention
- **I**nterest
- **D**esire
- **A**ction

AIDA principles apply to any sales letter. Format elements are:

- Hook
- Statement of problem/issue/situation
- Why your product/service is the answer
- Customer benefit (WIIFM)
- Action steps

II - DETERMINING FORMAT

I used to write advertising copy. One of the rules was that all copy should follow the AIDA principle. Create *A*ttention, *I*nterest, *D*esire and *A*ction. A sales letter employs that principle in the format that follows:

- A hook—something that triggers an emotional response from the customer, often painful or pleasurable, so they want to keep on reading to see if your product/service will really help them
- A statement of the problem/issue/situation that exists in the marketplace which the customer would like to have solved or benefit from
- Why your product/service is the answer
- Benefits to the customer (WIIFM—What's In It For Me)
- Action steps—by the customer and by you

These five elements often interact. For example, the hook might easily be part of the problem/issue/situation that exists in the marketplace. The product/service is often connected to benefits to the customer.

Where should you begin?

The problem/issue/situation that exists in the marketplace sets the stage for everything else that goes into your letter, including the hook. It is therefore the best place to begin thinking about and planning your sales letter. Many people try to come up with the hook before they've done this basic work. They might or might not get it right.

My experience is that the hook may be one of the last things to be finalized, often falling into place once the other pieces of the letter are established.

Be clear about the problem, issue or situation in the marketplace so that you can accurately position your product/service

Zephyr Scenario: **Problem/issue/situation**

The basic issue is that for some reason a printer isn't printing, a file won't load, a drive won't work, and it has to be fixed.

More important, the underlying issue is two-pronged:

1. Who can I turn to right now to get up and running?
2. I have to get this work done and out to my customer.

So the issue in the marketplace is:

"How can I find someone who I can call and get my computer problems fixed, right now, so I can get on with my work?"

Zephyr's promise is:

"We're as close as your phone. If you have a problem we'll fix it—8 to 8 weekdays, 8 to noon Saturdays."

The problem/issue/situation that exists in the marketplace

Many people, when writing sales letters, go straight to a sales pitch for their particular product or service. What they fail to explain is why there is a need for their product or service in the first place. They assume that you know, or will figure it out. My reaction is, why would anybody try to persuade me to buy something if they didn't first tell me why I would need it? Let me give you an example.

A woman in one of my seminars made beautiful wedding gowns. In her initial letter she wrote -

"If you'd like to have the most wonderful wedding gown, then I'm the person you ought to see."

What's wrong with that? Nothing, except that it doesn't get at the true need or issue in the marketplace. Does this describe what she does? Yes. Does it give a sense of extraordinary ability? Not necessarily. We suggested that she look at her business from the customer's point of view. Here's a bride on the most important day of her life. She wants to look wonderful, radiant, and above all, free of worry and care.

So we came up with a different approach.What you do, we said, is help make your client's wedding day one that she will always remember and cherish. So the issue or problem to be resolved in the marketplace is "How does a bride make sure that her gown, on this, the most wonderful day of her life, is something that she can count on?" The promise statement to resolve the issue is something like:

"We promise that you will receive, on time, an extraordinary wedding gown to crown the most wonderful day of your life."

With Zephyr Computer Services, the situation is that something's gone wrong with a client's computer system. They don't know how to fix it. What they do know is that they have to get this financial data out to some investors today and they're in panic mode. How Zephyr sees the problem/issue/situation in the marketplace is set out on the page opposite.

Why your product/service will resolve the problem, issue or situation:

- Why you're better
- The promises you'll keep
- Your track record
- Endorsements/testimonials

Zephyr Scenario: **Why Zephyr is the answer**

- Zephyr's partners have a combined experience of over 50 years in computer servicing, particularly for small- and medium-sized contracting businesses
- They will solve your problems 8 to 8 weekdays and 8 to noon Saturdays
- They will educate your people as to what went wrong and show them, where possible, how to fix it themselves
- They recruit staff internationally—clients always get people with the broadest experience and expertise

Here's another example. Financial planners/advisors who provide personal retirement planning. What's the issue or problem here? One way to state it is as follows "At age 65 only 5% of us will have enough funds to enjoy life the way we'd like to. Will you be one of them?"

The promise is something like ***"Choose us as your investment advisor and we'll help you to a worry-free financial retirement."***

You must understand and state the problem/issue/situation that people desire to have resolved or benefit from. If you understand, says the customer, then perhaps I will come to you for the solution. You must now convince the customer that your solution is better than anyone else's.

Why your product/service is the answer to resolving the problem/issue/situation

To prove that your company is the best qualified to resolve the problem/issue/situation in the marketplace, you must:

- Show what makes you new, better and different
- Show that you can deliver on your promises
- Give clients your track record (testimonials, third party endorsements)—what clients have said about you

Example. My clients tell me that my wedding gowns are among the best they've ever seen. They like the fact that I really listen when they describe what they want. I've won awards in Bride Magazine.

Example. We deliver lighting that is not only more efficient and long lasting, but cost effective. It cuts both operating and maintenance costs. And the lighting itself is as good as or better than higher priced systems.

With the Zephyr Computer Services scenario, you will see a number of strengths that support its position. To those strengths would be added any testimonials or endorsements from current or past clients.

Customer wants to know "What's In It For Me?" (WIIFM?)

Two basic elements:

- What benefit will I gain?
- What loss or pain will I avoid?

Zephyr Scenario: **Benefits to clients**

- Solid assurance that help is a phone call away when problems arise—8 to 8 weekdays and 8 to noon Saturdays
- We'll get you back to work, likely sooner than you think
- We'll educate you as to the problem so that next time you may not need to call us but can fix it yourselves

Benefits to the customer

This is the WIIFM—"What's In It For Me?" Sometimes it becomes difficult to separate out *benefits to the customer* from the previous step—*why your product/service is the answer to resolving the problem/issue/situation*. The one is often part of the other.

I prefer to separate out the benefits so that the customer is clear about why using your service or product is to their advantage. Here are some examples:

Example. When you use us as your investment advisor you'll have the financial resources you'll need when you retire. We'll also suggest some strategies that may reduce your tax liability.

Example. Purchase a new lighting system from us and you'll get great lighting to show off your product lines. Your electrical bills will be lower because our system uses less power. You'll replace tubes/bulbs less often.

Example. When you decide to buy your wedding gown from me you can be sure that you will look stunning. You will have absolute certainty that every stage from design to completion will be done on time, to your complete satisfaction. You will never have to worry about your gown not being ready when you need it.

These examples show the following respectively:

a. How the customer (here the consumer) will be able to avoid the pain of retiring and have the resources to live a good life
b. The benefits of saving money on the product and its operating costs—and how this lighting equipment will better display the company's product lines
c. The bride will not have to worry about her wedding gown, how wonderful it will look or whether it will be ready on time as promised. Notice how the copy stresses the gain (the joy of how stunning the bride will look in this wonderful gown) and avoidance of pain (a guarantee that the gown will be there on time as promised)

Take action

- Ask for the order
- Encourage customers to get back to you by providing:
  - clear contact information
  - incentives
  - convenience, such as easy reply envelopes and toll free numbers

Zephyr Scenario: **Incentive**

We offer you a free consultation to determine how well your computer systems are working. Any problems that we can fix there and then will be done at no charge. This offer is valid through April 30th.

Simply circle "Yes, I want to take advantage of your special free consultation" and fax it back to us, or e-mail us.

Action steps

In advertising terminology this is the ***call to action***. There are three elements to consider:

1. Asking for the order
2. How will the customer get back to you?
3. How will you follow up with the customer?

1. Asking for the order

Asking for the order is a step that some of us are uneasy about. But then, why write a sales letter and leave out its raison d'être? Whether it's to buy motor oil, design a wedding gown or hire a financial advisor, the request needs to be in the letter.

With Zephyr Computer Services it's simple—"We want to be your computer service people. To encourage you, we'll give you a service check of your systems at no charge." The offer gives Zephyr the opportunity to build both their client base and their relationship with the client.

2. How will the customer get back to you?

Basic contact information. Give the customer clear information on your mailing address, phone, fax, e-mail, web site, your place of business or a store carrying your product. (Many web sites fail to provide this contact information easily.)

Give them an incentive. Use incentives to encourage customers to get back to you.

- If you're a consultant you might want to make that initial consultation a complimentary one
- Give away product samples, or a price incentive
- Buy before April 30 and get 20% off the regular price, or buy one at the regular price, get a second one free

Make it convenient. Customers are more likely to act if you:

- Provide easy to fill out, reply information
- Enclose a business reply envelope and a business card with your letter
- Provide a toll free number to place an order

Make sure you follow up:

- By phone
- In person
- By letter, e-mail or fax

My experience is that people appreciate when you take the time to follow up. They may not use you now, but they do remember. That can be of exceptional value for future opportunities.

Zephyr Scenario: **Follow up**

- We will follow up with you within the next two weeks to make sure you have received this letter and to schedule an appointment to check your systems.

3. How will you follow up with the customer?

If you know the name of the person and/or the company, state that you will contact them either:

- By phone:
  - you can expect a call from us in 10 days
  - I will contact you by the end of the month
- In person:
  - one of our representatives will call at your office within the next three weeks
  - I'll call to make an appointment at a mutually convenient time

By making this commitment you're giving your letter some teeth. Customers know you will call. They know they will have to make a decision about your product or service one way or another. One follow up call may not do it. It often takes three, four, five or more. You could also follow up with a letter or e-mail or fax, outlining additional information or incentives the customer should know about or can act upon.

In the Zephyr Scenario, if there's been no response within a couple of weeks, you'd get on the phone and find out whether the letter was received in the first place. If it was, ask whether you can book a free consultation. If not received, send them another letter and follow that up.

Marketing imperative—make sure you follow up!

I can't end this section without stressing the importance of follow up. Before my partner sold her travel business, I regularly made calls to see if those to whom we sent travel information (a) received it, (b) had any questions we could answer, and (c) decided whether to book. It never ceased to amaze me how many people valued the call. It didn't matter whether they had a question, or whether they had decided not to go. They appreciated that we kept our word, wanted us to keep in touch, and remembered us next time.

If you can't, for whatever reason, make the call when you say, do it later. People understand that sometimes circumstances get in the way. Apologize for the delay and go from there. If you come across as sincere, people will almost always go halfway to meet you.

The hook

Strike an emotional chord with the customer:

- We can solve your problem and get rid of any pain or concern you feel about a situation
- You will really benefit from our product or service

If you have problems coming up with a hook, move on to other parts of the sales letter. The hook will fall in place later.

Zephyr Scenario: **Possible hook**

"Is there anything worse than a system that breaks down just when you have to get a critical job to a customer?"

A quick word about using the phone. These days we are inundated with telemarketing calls. If you ***cold call***, make sure that your tone is warm and polite—and avoid the awful scripting so prevalent in phone pitches. Be natural. The key is your confidence in your own product or service...and if you can promise to keep the call brief, 30 seconds to a minute, people are more likely to hear you out.

The hook

The hook must spark the customer's interest by striking some kind of emotional chord dealing with either pain or pleasure. The product or service will solve a difficult situation, avoid a loss, or make you feel good. The hook tells you that you can save money...prevent disease... buy the same item at lower cost, etc.

For example, if you are a financial advisor and you want to stress paying less tax, your hook might be:

"You can reduce the taxes you pay now and have more income when you retire. We'll show you how." Or, "I can save you an average of $1,500 annually on your taxes."

The lighting manufacturer might say:

"One single light fixture can cut your lighting budget by $100 a year. Imagine what ten or more can do!"

The hook is designed to grab attention and then, very importantly, flow into the sales letter itself. The hook might also be part of the opening section of your letter dealing with the issue to be resolved in the marketplace. In this case a separate hook may not be required.

On the opposite page is the kind of hook that customers for Zephyr Computer Services might respond to.

If you have problems coming up with a hook, move on. Deal with the other parts of the sales letter first.

Next steps

With the elements of the format established, you are ready to begin assembling your letter. It's time to write.

Plan the letter

First, think about what you're wanting to accomplish

Next, follow the format:

- Hook
- Define the problem/issue/ situation in the marketplace
- Why you can solve it
- Benefit to the customer
- Action steps—by you and the customer

Need more help? Try:

- Chunking
- Mind mapping
- Freewriting

III - WRITING & REVISING

You know what you need to cover in the letter. I suggest that you follow the format as your pathway or outline. To remind you, that format or pathway goes as follows:

- What is the hook?
- What is the problem/issue/situation in the marketplace that needs to be resolved?
- Why are you/your company right for the task?
- What is the benefit to the customer (WIIFM)?
- What action steps are required?

A question you may want to keep in mind is this: is there a separate hook at the start of the letter? If not, how does the hook fit into the opening sentence?

Some thoughts before you write

Before you start writing, give yourself some time to think about the letter and what it entails. Things may start to fall in place in your mind. At that stage you may be able to write a reasonable letter covering all the points. Failing that, you might want to try one of the following:

- Working in chunks
- Mind mapping
- Freewriting

Working in chunks

What I often do is write a first cut to the whole letter. Then, I take a small section or chunk and work it intensely. I'll play around with it until I'm satisfied. I'll do the same with the other parts of the letter—again until I'm satisfied. I'll then look to see if the individual chunks I've created still flow together or if I have to do any bridging between them.

Mind mapping

I may do a mind map, particularly if what I'm writing is longer than a page or two. The mind map allows me to get out all the ideas for the letter. I might see where things are missing or what connections there are between the various elements. If you try this, you'll find that by prioritizing the elements for each part of the format, you give yourself an outline to follow to write the letter itself.

Zephyr Scenario: **Sales letter freewrite**

We know that you are very concerned when your computers break down to have it fixed right away. Well we're quite literally as close as a phone call—so please call us—we can get there right away and nine times out of ten we can fix the problem right away.

How can we guarantee that? Well there are five of us here and we're hiring new people to keep up with the workload. One of us will be able to get there—if not we'll make sure that someone's there by the end of the day. But because we've been in the construction industry, we know some of the problems you're likely to be facing.

We keep ourselves up to date—in fact we get to seminars at least twice a year and we are certified by all the leading manufacturers—so it doesn't matter what equipment you have.

We're always reachable because we have a mobile phone system that allows us all to keep in touch and know where our people are at—so if one of us can't get there we can find out who is available.

We want to encourage you to use us. Our existing clients keep telling us to have people who are thinking about using us call them - actually we're thinking of doing an open house at our place—we want to invite you to our workplace on March 28—we'll have enough refreshments for everyone—but it'll be an opportunity to meet us—we'll have some of our present clients there so you can ask them questions if you want…ask us questions—and when you're back in your office we'll follow up with you and see if you'd like us to be your back up. And you can tell us what your biggest concerns are and we'll see if we can address them for you.

If you're stuck you have several options:

- Write what you know
- Take a break
- Ask someone for advice

You must start writing!

Freewriting

Freewriting can be very useful. If you've got a lot of thoughts spinning around in your head, get them out by writing them down—then, see what you've got. Does it contain all the elements that are important in the letter?

Take a highlighter and mark those elements that belong in the letter. Next, incorporate them into the actual letter when you do your first draft.

If you look at the freewrite opposite developed for Zephyr Computer Services, it has most elements already sequenced appropriately. You'd check to see what should be part of the actual letter, what needs restating or correcting, and what might still be missing.

What if you're stuck?

Sometimes writing's easy. It flows – five steps, all in a row. But sometimes you get stuck. What am I going to say, you wonder, as you drink your third cup of coffee?

I suggest to clients that they write what they know. If you know what your product will do, start with that. If you know what the benefits are to the customer, do that instead. Then go back and work on the other parts.

You could also take a break, or ask someone else for advice.

As soon as you can, start writing. Thinking will only get you so far. Somewhere you have to get pen to paper, or fingers working the keyboard. Once there, the writing itself often becomes easier.

First draft

- Check for completeness and accuracy of content
- Is audience convinced that you:
  - understand the issue?
  - can resolve it?
  - can deliver the benefits?
- Is tone and manner right for this audience?
- General considerations:
  - keep it personal
  - avoid jargon
  - simple not complex (KISS)
  - active not passive
  - positive not negative
- Tell the truth:
  - crucial to building relationships
- Make sure the letter flows:
  - read it out loud
  - does it flow from one section to another?
  - focus test it with colleagues or friends

YOU'VE WRITTEN A FIRST DRAFT

Once you've got a first draft, check what you've written. Start with **content**:

- Have you identified the issue in the marketplace?
- Have you convinced the reader that your product or service will resolve the issue?
- Have you spelled out the benefits the customer gains from buying your product, using your service, or supporting a cause you promote?
- Have you told the customer how to take advantage of this opportunity? Can they contact you easily? Is there an incentive for them to do so? Is there a time limit on what you may be offering?
- Have you told the customer how you will follow up with them?

Tone and manner of the letter

Know your audience and write for them

To whom are you writing? Academics, engineers, business people? Information Technology (IT) people? Seniors? Students? General public? Young mothers? Fitness buffs?

Where you can, keep the letter:

- Personal—we like to be talked to one on one, not talked at
- Free of jargon, unless the terminology is familiar to your audience
- Simple rather than complex (the KISS principle—Keep It Simple)
- Active not passive; e.g., "The sales department set up a trip to Spain," rather than, "A trip to Spain was set up by the sales department."
- Positive not negative; e.g., "You'll have a great night's sleep thanks to our security systems," rather than, "You won't stay awake all night worrying if you're safe."

Tell the truth

You are building a relationship with a customer. You want them to trust you so that they keep coming back and refer you to others.

Make sure your letter flows

- Read it out loud
- Does it flow easily from one section to another?
- You might want to ***focus test*** it with friends or colleagues and ask for their feedback

- Length of the letter:
  - preferably shorter
  - depends on complexity of your product/service
  - whatever works—as long as the writing involves the audience and moves them to act

Appearance

- Make the hook your impact point
- Divide the letter into clean blocks of sentences
- Keep overall column narrower for easier reading
- Left justify only
- Use white space

Illustration

- Use graphics and images only if they enhance the letter and are cost effective

Length of the letter

Generally, people prefer shorter letters. They only have so much time to read and don't want to be bothered with something that takes up too much of it. I noticed recently that letters from charitable organizations tend to be a couple of pages, back to back. They often get into a touching story and in that way grab people's emotions.

If the subject matter is complex, then the letter may realistically require several pages for explanation.

The real answer to length of letter, however, is whatever works. If it's interesting to the audience, even though it takes longer to explain, it may be absolutely fine. You have to determine that.

The letter's appearance

Appearance is simply making sure that the way the letter looks reflects the content that you wish to communicate.

The hook is always the most important focus of your letter. Customers will only care about your name, or your logo, if they find you have something of value to offer them. The hook should therefore stand out as the place to which the eye is first drawn. Of course that hook could be a photograph or graphic of some kind, rather than a headline.

What is important is that each section of the letter follows smoothly from the section before. Now it helps if these sections are in blocks of sentences or paragraphs rather than one continuous piece of writing. The customer can then distinguish between the points you are making. They can see that you understand their problem, have a solution to help them, and will benefit from using you.

I want to add three points about readability:

Keep the column of writing narrower. If a column or page is narrower, it tends to be an easier read. The eye doesn't have to move as much.

Left justify only. Full justification often means odd spacing.

More white space. Don't jam up the letter. Keep it open. More white space makes for an easier, more relaxed read.

Graphics and pictures

Should you use graphics to illustrate a point in a letter? If a graphic tells the story better than words, use it! That little bit of extra effort may produce a few more customers. On the other hand, if the only thing that's going to sell the product is price and a limited time offer, keep graphics to a minimum or don't use them. The determining factor is how great a difference will it make to results? Is it cost effective?

February 25, 2004

James Rademayer
Eastern Contracting
1702 Cary Blvd.
Los Angeles, CA
90027

Dear James:

Thank you for speaking with me yesterday. This is a follow up to the question I raised…

> ***"You have a deadline you have to meet when all of a sudden the printer has an inexplicable time out, or you can't load a file that worked fine yesterday…"***

James, what does your company do when this happens—when the job is critical and you wonder where to turn to get back on track in a hurry? Well if you're faced with this kind of problem, we're the people you want at the end of the phone. We can do something about it—weekdays 8 to 8 and Saturdays 8 to noon.

There are five of us here at Zephyr Computer Services. Individually we've been involved in this business since 1994—that's over 50 years of combined experience. We formed Zephyr six months ago in order to provide better service to you the client than we could on our own.

If you ask our current clients—see the attached testimonials—they'll tell you that we work in two ways. The first is we'll always fix the problem so you can get back to work. Second, we'll help you understand what's going on so if it happens again, you might be able to solve things before we get there—or not even need us at all.

Because we'd like to introduce ourselves in person, we want to make you a special offer—we'll check your system at our expense. If we see something that needs fixing and we can do it easily, we'll repair it at no charge. If we can't, we'll tell you what's involved then let you decide whether you want us to do it for you. This offer is good for the next two months through the end of April. Just check the space at the foot of this letter and fax it back to us. Or simply send us an e-mail.

We will, in any event, give you a call in a couple of weeks to make sure you received this letter and see if there's anything we can help you with. In the meantime, our thanks, and please enjoy the copy of our latest e-mail newsletter in which we keep our clients up to speed with what's happening in the market.

We want your business. Call us any time you have a systems problem you cannot resolve. We'll be there. And take advantage of our special offer. We mean it!

With kind regards,

Helen Reiner

……… Yes, I want Zephyr Computer Services to check our systems.

Zephyr Computer Services

33 Grosvenor Place, Unit 17, Santa Monica, CA, 90041
Tel: 234 777-2120 Fax: 234 777-2121
e-mail: zcs@pacific.net

REVISING THE LETTER

Once you've taken a good look at your first draft, read it several times and had others look at it, it's time to go for a second draft and perhaps the final version.

How many drafts should you write?

There's no cut and dried answer to this question. Since letters are usually not too long, there's less time involved in trying out different versions. You can therefore do as many drafts as you want, within reason and your timeline. Feel free to play around with what you've got until you're comfortable with it. In particular, try putting yourself in your customer's (or consumer's) shoes. What do you think their reaction will be to your letter? Is it what you intend?

You can also show revised drafts to others to get their reactions.

On the opposite page is a final version of the letter from Zephyr Computer Services to their potential customer.

Completion

The tough part of writing a sales letter is often the question of letting go. There comes a time when you must simply stop revising the letter and send it out. That's completion. So do your best, and let it go.

Reports

Reports give us the information we need in order to make informed choices

Reports may:

- Clarify situations
- Assess alternative courses of action
- Provide feedback
- Reflect a current position

Characteristics

A report:

- Is often a written analysis of an issue or situation to help someone make a decision
- May be based on facts alone, or facts backed by informed opinion
- May require conclusions and recommendations

WHAT IS A REPORT?

Reports serve many different purposes. They're used in deciding whether to open a new business or determining if a language class is justified in a new school. They can ***report*** on the results of a trade show, the progress of a customer survey, or whether it's viable to convert an old warehouse to upscale lofts. They may come in the form of annual reports, reflecting on an organization's performance over the past year. They may be production reports, detailing items manufactured this week, this month or this quarter.

More than anything else, reports give us the information we need in order to make informed choices. If a decision has to be made, reports clarify situations, assess alternative courses of action, draw conclusions, and where appropriate, give recommendations.

Definition and purpose

How do you define a report, given that there are many different types? One way to describe a report is:

A written analysis of an issue or situation

The purpose of a report based on this definition is usually to help someone make a decision. For example, to persuade an organization to move in a different direction, invest in a computer network, develop new products or spend money on research.

In many cases, however, a report may simply be the presentation of information with no decision required; e.g., a report on the results of a sales trip.

A report may be based on facts alone, or facts backed up by informed opinion, leading to conclusions, often supported by recommendations.

Reports that provide the needed information clearly, in an easily digestible format, help organizations make the right choices.

A report is often the best way for management to:

- Obtain an analysis of a particular issue or situation
- Get specific information by a deadline

How a report gets generated

The board or management of an organization often face issues or situations that need to be resolved. A report is the most common and comprehensive way for the results of a study, or analysis of an issue or situation, to be presented to that board or management. It may also be the best way for the board or management to get information by a deadline. They may assign the task to one of their own members. However, with constraints on time, resources and expertise they often assign it elsewhere, either within the organization or to outside consultants.

If you are an entrepreneur or small business, you will almost certainly develop a business plan. A key component of that plan may be a marketing strategy report to determine the best ways to market your product or service.

How this report section is broken down

There are six parts:

Part I - Types of report

Part II - Planning & research

Part III - Analyzing what you've got

Part IV - Writing the report

Part V - Packaging the report

Part VI - Writing considerations

In developing a report you will likely find yourself moving around between sections as the need arises. For example, you may find it easier to analyze a particular piece of information prior to planning because what you find will impact the planning itself.

Feel free, therefore, to go through this section and select the areas that are more important to you.

Progress/Interim reports

Assess the current status of a particular project or process

- Is the project on track?
- Is it worth continuing?
- Allows issues to be thoroughly discussed and evaluated

To: Jean Marsden, Chair, Woodlance County Board
From: Ray Ramirez, Director of Project Planning
Date: April 4, 2004
Subject: Woodlance Library Project - #05-2004

Here is the March 31, 2004 progress report on the Woodlance Library Project that began on February 7, 2004.

Reconstruction
2nd floor newspaper and magazine section

- Books and periodicals temporarily relocated to the 1st floor
- The contractor has stripped all ceiling tiles and electrical fixtures in preparation for the installation of new lighting and air conditioning
- Electrical work for the area is on time and on budget
- A three week delay is being experienced in installing new air conditioning ducts due to (a) structural problems on site and (b) supply of materials

1st floor children's section

- Slated for relocation beginning April 10
- Ceiling to be stripped in preparation for new electrical and air conditioning

The contractor has assured us that air conditioning work in the children's section will be coordinated with that in the newspaper/magazine section. As a result, the current delays in installing air conditioning are expected to be resolved.

Installation of new book inventory system

- The schedule for the installation of the new book inventory system has been approved by library staff and the supplier
- Shipment of new terminals will begin in the last week of April

Funding

- We have received the 1/3 payment ($75,000) from the Carlaw Foundation
- We are still awaiting the first payment from the City of Woodlance. The Director of Finance has promised a reply by April 8. The city is currently focused on budget negotiations and that is taking priority at this time

Summary

Overall, the project is proceeding as planned. However we are concerned that:

- Funding is provided on time as promised by the city
- The contractor's air conditioning issues do not delay the project

Our staff are closely monitoring both these issues.

I - TYPES OF REPORT

There are several types of report, with different names, such as feasibility report, technical report, annual report, and financial report. The ones considered here are:

- Progress/Interim reports
- Information reports
- Analytical reports

Progress/Interim reports

These reports assess how a particular project or process is progressing. For example:

- A building under construction—what stage is it at?
- A report on the need for English as a Second Language (ESL) programs for new citizens. What is its status?

Conclusions and/or recommendations may or may not be asked for. The results are used to determine whether:

1. **You are on the right track**
   Is the project headed in the right direction? Is this investment of money, time and other resources appropriate? If a correction or adjustment is needed, it may be better to do it now rather than later. It's therefore important to keep the board or management involved in the project's progress, and prepare them if the findings are not what was hoped for.
2. **The project is worth pursuing**
   It's not always clear whether a project is worth doing. The status quo, or a different course of action altogether, might be better. Now is the time to find out.

Progress/Interim reports provide an opportunity for issues to be thoroughly discussed with others. Those who hired you can review what you've found and either concur, disagree, or suggest a change of direction.

On the opposite page you will see an example of a progress report and the kind of format followed.

Information reports

- A snapshot in time—it tells us what has taken place in a given situation

To: Roger Verlay
From: Carole Rennie
Date: November 26, 2004
Re: World Travel Mart, London

I spent three days at the World Travel Mart (WTM) in London from November 10-12. It was a very busy, productive visit. I will have full details to present to you next week. However, as requested, here are the highlights.

European tours status
I spoke with incoming tour operators for Spain, Italy and Scandinavia. As well as picking up material from their respective booths, they will be supplying us with a number of options for our planned 21-day, 14-day and special long weekend European tours.

High end safaris
I spent considerable time in the African section at WTM in line with our proposed entry into the safari market for high end travelers. Again I picked up material and will be receiving detailed information from a number of suppliers to evaluate. These will be suitable for both our tour groups and for individual travelers.

Other travel opportunities
Prior to going to WTM we had discussed the possibility of further extending the adventure travel component of our business. Several unique possibilities exist for guided river and wildlife tours in South America and East Africa. WTM gave me the opportunity to sit down with two suppliers who focus on the Amazon and Madagascar respectively. Both take small groups with professional guides and qualified naturalists. I have both the tour details and tentative rates.

I will be organizing the material I brought back over the next few days and would like to make a detailed presentation to all staff later next week.

Analytical reports

Deal with areas such as:

- An unworkable situation
- Uncertainty on how to proceed with a particular issue
- Advice on strategic planning

Information reports

Rather like a snapshot in time, information reports include such reports as annual reports, sales reports and product inventory. These reports set out what has taken place in a given situation; e.g., share values holding steady; sales up 30%; inventory levels are too high.

Information reports do not normally require conclusions and recommendations. This is not to say that you won't be asked for your opinion on the results.

On the page opposite is an example of an information report—it literally gives you that snapshot in time. What happened when? The report will be used for some kind of decision, even if it's a decision to do nothing.

Analytical reports

These are the reports (also called interpretive reports) that require the most from the persons asked to write them. They are ***cause and effect*** reports or ***what if*** scenarios. You're probably told ***Here's the situation. Here's what we'd like to know. Here's what we'd like to see. How do we get there?*** Your task is to check out the situation. You research to gather appropriate information. You then analyze that situation, draw conclusions and make recommendations.

These reports will most likely revolve around business situations, such as strategic planning, marketing, manufacturing and fiscal. For example:

- Should we consider moving into other markets?
- Should we expand our IT network?
- Should we stop manufacturing this item?
- How do our customers see us?
- How should we reorganize our shipping program?

> The focus in the report section is on analytical reports requested by management—those that require research, analysis, conclusions and recommendations whose length is from short (2-3 pages) to medium (20-30 pages).

Form of report

- Memo or letter (brief report) e.g. progress and information reports
- Semi-formal (mid length) e.g. analytical reports
- Formal (usually longer reports that deal with complex issues and analytical in nature)

The following Lease/Buy Scenario is used throughout the report section to illustrate the development of an analytical report:

The medium-sized construction company, Goertz Construction & Development, has hired your consulting firm. The company owns a dozen vehicles. Six of these are pick-up trucks—4 light duty and 2 heavy duty with special equipment. The pick-ups need to be replaced over the next two years. You have been asked to report on whether it's better to buy, as in the past, or lease the new vehicles. No elaborate report is asked for, simply the facts, your conclusions and recommendations. It shouldn't take you more than 4-5 pages. The owner of the company would like to have the report in two weeks.

What form should your report take?

There are several different forms of report. Some are short, like a memo or letter. For example, progress reports and information reports are often quite brief, set out as an inter office memo or a letter directed to the individual or group of people who need to see them.

Analytical reports tend to be longer. For example, research findings from a series of interviews or surveys require clear documentation, helped by appropriate graphics and tables. These might be a dozen pages or more. Others can be several hundred pages, such as a government report on health care. A report might also take the form of a newsletter or a manual.

Much depends on what those who requested the report are looking for. A colleague reminds me that many people simply want a report to be "*quick and dirty*"—a few pages only—just information on which to make a decision.

Next steps

How do you go about developing your report? The first thing you do is plan, and prepare for the research that may be necessary.

The purpose statement

- What is the objective of this report?

> Lease/Buy Scenario: **Purpose statement**
>
> "Determine the best option for acquiring new vehicles, either lease or purchase."

Other terms of reference

- Report parameters, deadlines, budget and resources

> Lease/Buy Scenario: **Terms of reference**
>
> - Research the cost of leasing or buying new vehicles over the next 6 to 12 month period
> - Provide options for management to be able to make a decision
> - Make and model of trucks already selected
> - Provide your analysis, conclusions and recommendations
> - A mix of buy and lease is an acceptable option
> - Talk to anyone in the company you need to—they have been instructed to provide full cooperation
> - This must not be an elaborate report—just sufficient for us to see the information and to be able to make a decision
> - You have a budget of $500 for expenses, if required, to talk to people or research information
> - No interim draft is required
> - You may talk to any experts, banks, dealers to get their input

II - PLANNING & RESEARCH

The planning and research process requires answers to three questions:

1. What are your terms of reference?
2. Who is your audience and what do they need to know?
3. How will you plan and research your report?

1. What are your terms of reference?

You need to be clear about the terms of reference (also called *criteria* or *parameters*) so that your report is always focused and meets the need of the target audience. It's useful to break the terms of reference into three areas:

- Purpose statement
- Other terms of reference
- Limitations

Purpose statement

The purpose statement is the driver for everything you do. It incorporates the key elements and answers the question ***Why has this report been asked for and what is its objective?*** Keeping the purpose statement in front of you at all times helps to ensure that your work stays on track.

Other terms of reference

The information required below completes the terms of reference for the report:

- Knowing whether the report:
  - is simply reporting on a situation
  - has a broad or narrow focus
  - requires analysis, conclusions and recommendations
  - needs interim reports or drafts
- The deadline
- The budget
- Resources available, such as staff, equipment and technology
- Latitude given to author/s of the report

Be careful in making assumptions

Report limitations

- Budget
- Time
- Information:
  - is unavailable
  - too costly
  - no time to obtain
- Resources not available

Know your audience

- Who reads the report?
- Who acts on it?
- How informed are they?
- Is technical language okay?
- Kind of report expected?

Watch your assumptions. Don't begin a report without determining the terms of reference, your understanding of them, and verifying that your understanding is correct. Which leads immediately to the danger of making assumptions. Assume nothing! Some reports have specific instructions as to content guidelines. Many don't. Others have informal guidelines, often the result of conversations of which you may be unaware. Check it out!

Limitations

Are there limitations that might affect your report, such as:

- Budget—funding is limited
- Time—we need it by July 15th and it's now July 10th
- Information may be unavailable because of cost, time, or it simply doesn't exist
- Resources—people are unavailable, or research has been delayed

Limitations may be open to negotiation if you can show that additional research or more resources will significantly impact the report's value and/or improve decision making.

2. *Who is your audience and what do they need to know?*

No one wants to prepare a report only to discover that the audience is unable to understand it or use it. For a report that works for the reader, these questions need answers:

- Who will read your report? Who will act on your report? Are they the same or different audiences?
- How informed is your audience? How much should you tell them, given their understanding of the situation?
- Will the language you use cause any misunderstanding due to technical, scientific, or other reasons? If so, might they consider your work unsatisfactory or find themselves unable to make an informed decision?
- What form of the report will best serve this audience? A rush job with a fast decision may mean putting it together in a form that quickly emphasizes key points by using bullets

Help your audience

- Provide the information they need
- Show that you understand the situation and objective
- Support your research with facts and/or qualified opinion
- Provide easy to follow conclusions/recommendations

Lease/Buy Scenario: **Audience**

- The audience is the management team, with strong emphasis on the owner whose opinion carries a lot of weight
- They are a well-informed group
- It must be an easy read with conclusions and recommended options
- Use bullets and tables where appropriate
- The owner gives you full permission to be proactive and look for alternatives that might not normally be considered

Planning and researching your report

The information you'll need

- Use purpose statement as guide
- Develop a skeleton outline (try using a mind map)

Help your audience

Make it easy for your audience to read and understand your report. Here's what an audience member might tell you:

- I have too much to read. Give me the information I need to make a decision as quickly as possible
- Show me that you understand the situation and the objective
- Assure me that all the necessary research has been done and back up your findings with facts supported by opinions, qualifying any assumptions you make
- Make it easy for me to draw conclusions
- Give me recommendations based on your expertise
- Don't give me information that I don't need or want
- Put information you think I should have access to, but don't need in the body of the report, into an appendix. I can read it if I choose

3. How will you plan and research your report?

You're clear about your purpose statement. You're clear who your audience is. You now focus on a plan to bring it to reality. It starts with the answers to these questions:

- What information do I need?
- How will I get the information?

What information do I need?

Keep the purpose statement in front of you

The purpose statement drives your need for information. To remind you, here is the one for the Lease/Buy Scenario:

> ***"Determine the best option for acquiring new vehicles, either lease or purchase."***

Give yourself a preliminary skeleton of your outline

When you begin a report, you have a pretty good idea of the areas you need to cover. It's therefore very useful to set up this skeleton. You can then attach information to each area as it gets generated.

Lease/Buy Scenario: **Information needed**

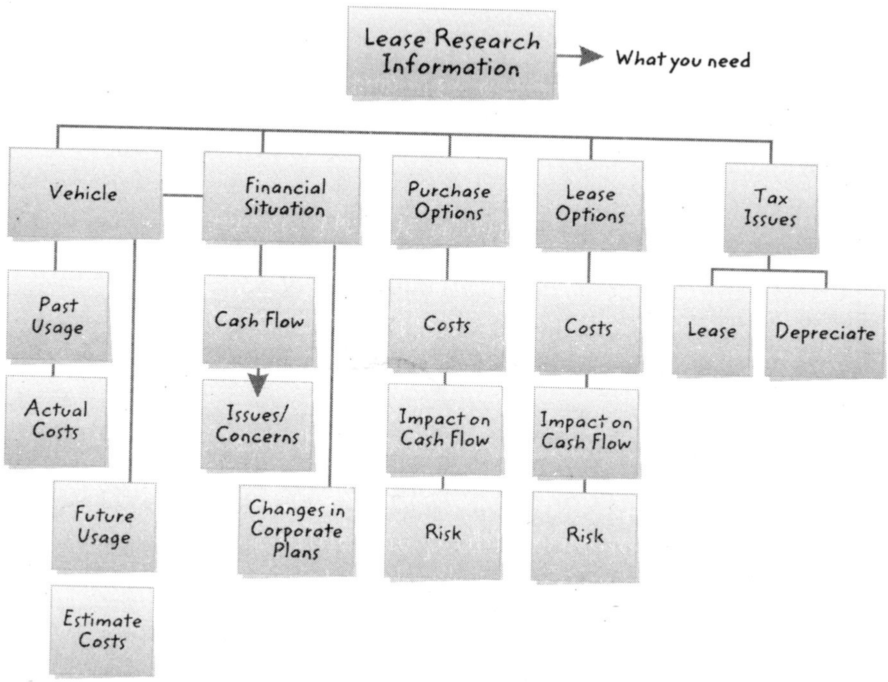

Where to find information

Primary sources
First-hand information—your own ideas and thinking, surveys, site visits, interviews, questionnaires

Secondary sources
Sources removed from you—books, magazines, newspapers, reports, journals, films, TV, Internet

It's probably easy enough to set out the areas you need to cover. If you're not sure, brainstorming and mind mapping can certainly help you. This was done with the Lease/Buy Scenario mind map on the opposite page:

- Vehicle itself—usage, desired life span, fuel and repair costs, warranties, trade-in values, etc.
- Lease options—rates based on usage, end of lease value, special fees, monthly payments
- Purchase options and costs—outright purchase, bank or dealer loan, deposit, interest rates
- Company's financial position and prospects—impact of cash flow on lease or purchase options
- Tax issues: is it more advantageous to write off annually as a lease or to take depreciation?

The five areas of the mind map could make up your skeleton. Further points of information that will require research and analysis are shown under appropriate columns.

How will I get the information?

Information comes from primary and secondary sources.

- **Primary sources**
  This is first-hand information, such as direct interaction through interviews, surveys you have conducted, site visits and most importantly, anything that comes from your own (or your team's) expertise and thinking.
- **Secondary sources**
  These are sources "removed" from you, where you are unlikely to have been involved in their creation; e.g., newspapers, books, magazines and journals, other reports, videos, films, TV, the Internet. *A **word of caution:*** resources such as Internet web sites are not necessarily current and up-to-date. Check any information to confirm accuracy of the source.

When mind mapping or brainstorming, don't try to separate primary and secondary sources. It interrupts your flow of thinking. (For more detailed information on primary and secondary sources, see page 67.)

Lease/Buy Scenario: **Where to find the information**

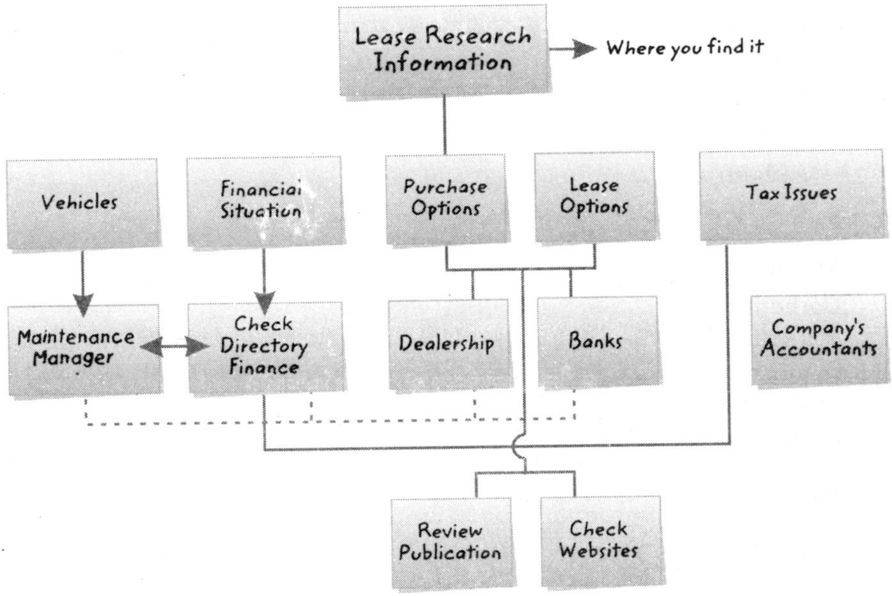

Organize your information

- Categorize for easy access to sources of data
- Reference your information to:
  - identify your sources
  - legitimize information
  - acknowledge expert source that validates your viewpoint

Information required by the Lease/Buy Scenario

The mind map opposite shows what information is required for the Lease/Buy Scenario and where to locate it. Using that mind map as a guide, specific information is developed as to where the required information may be found:

- Vehicle usage—check with the maintenance manager, operators, financial people
- Lease/purchase options—talk to dealerships, banks, other leasing companies
- Financial position—check with the director of finance
- Tax issues—check with the director of finance and/or tax authorities
- Review magazine articles for advice as well as check web sites

Tracking what you've got

Gathering information is one thing. Organizing it so you can find what you want is another. The problem is usually one of overload—I've got so much stuff, what am I going to do with it all? You might use binders, files and filing cabinets, index cards, a database, and maybe a great assistant to help you.

Referencing your sources

It's important to reference your sources so as to:

1. Identify the source as the provider of information
2. Provide legitimacy of information to readers. If they wish to check, they know where to find it
3. Acknowledge an expert source that has validated your point of view

- Listing your sources:
  - informal system
  - formal system; e.g. MLA/APA

Lease/Buy Scenario: **Information sources**

- Meeting with John Torres, maintenance manager re vehicle usage, costs & performance March 14, 17 & 18
- Meeting with Rachel Jameson, director of finance re cash flow projections, impact of expansion plans, tax issues & to assess lease and buy findings—March 15 & 22
- Meeting with Elaine Rodemayer, Horizon Bank lease manager re lease/buy—March 19
- Meeting with Al Purves and Graham Reese at Conway Motors re lease/buy—March 20
- Attached listing of web sites on lease/buy options—checked March 19
- Automotive Weekly, January 2002 issue page 38 "When leasing makes sense," by Arlene Walker

Listing your sources

Exactly how you list your sources depends on how formal or informal the report happens to be. If it's informal, you could simply record the sources as a series of bullets, as in the following example:

- Meeting of Finance Committee, March 13, 2004
- Interview with John Ryan, his office, March 17, 2004
- Research Department Planning Study, November 2002
- Article "What Researchers Get Paid" in Canadian Human Resources Journal, June 17, 2000 page 44
- Meeting with HR liaison committee, February 27, 2004
- Argon Research web site – www.argon.research.com
- Book "2001's best paying companies to work for" by James Frost and Freda Byrne

On the page opposite are the Lease/Buy Scenario sources.

A more formal process is to use a reference system that follows particular conventions in documenting authorship, date, title, publisher, etc. The appendix to this book provides a comparative reference guide for the MLA (Modern Language Association) and APA (American Psychological Association) systems.

Next steps

You've come up with the information you need in order to determine required courses of action. You now have to analyze that information to see what it tells you.

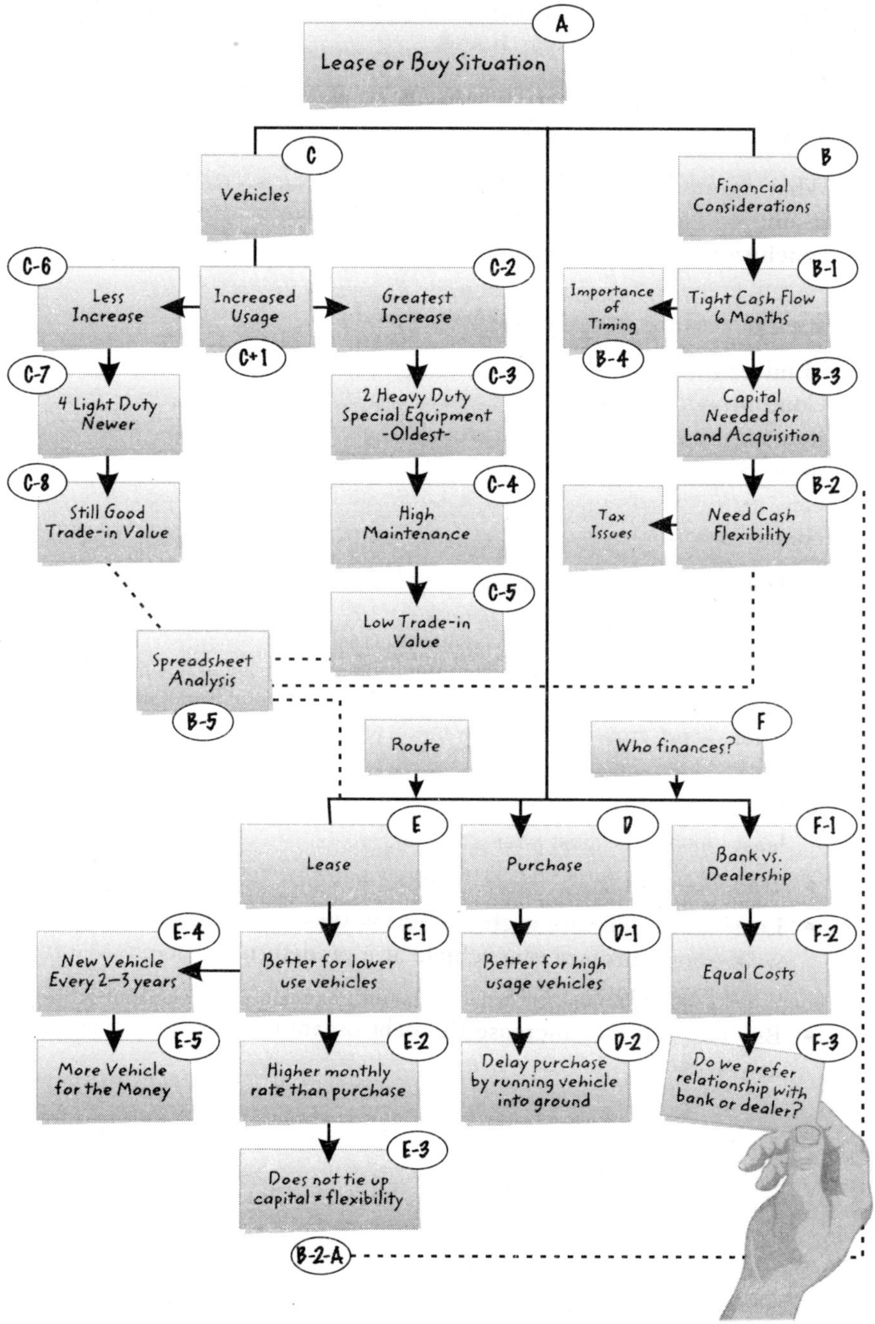

A
Lease or Buy Situation
C
Vehicles
B
Financial Considerations
C-6
Less Increase
Increased Usage
C+1
C-2
Greatest Increase
Importance of Timing
B-4
B-1
Tight Cash Flow 6 Months
C-7
4 Light Duty Newer
C-3
2 Heavy Duty Special Equipment -Oldest-
B-3
Capital Needed for Land Acquisition
C-8
Still Good Trade-in Value
C-4
High Maintenance
Tax Issues
B-2
Need Cash Flexibility
C-5
Low Trade-in Value
Spreadsheet Analysis
B-5
Route
F
Who finances?
E
Lease
D
Purchase
F-1
Bank vs. Dealership
E-4
New Vehicle Every 2–3 years
E-1
Better for lower use vehicles
D-1
Better for high usage vehicles
F-2
Equal Costs
E-5
More Vehicle for the Money
E-2
Higher monthly rate than purchase
D-2
Delay purchase by running vehicle into ground
F-3
Do we prefer relationship with bank or dealer?
E-3
Does not tie up capital = flexibility
B-2-A

III - ANALYZING WHAT YOU'VE GOT

This is where your skills come into play as you take all the information generated from your research and:

- Sort it into appropriate areas as per your skeleton
- Analyze what you've got

What does it tell you? What doesn't it tell you? What's missing? The results of your analysis become the basis on which to draw your conclusions and make recommendations.

Keep using exploration tools

Mind maps make it easier to determine where you are going. Continuing the Lease/Buy Scenario, on the opposite page you can see how information has been sorted. The priorities are identified on the mind map as B through F in sequence of importance with B-1, B-2, etc., as subheadings. Here are some of the important areas up for consideration:

- The company's financial situation will be tough for six months, then cash flow should start to improve
- Lease payments would be higher than loan payments
- Maintenance people say it's best to keep repairing the heavy duty trucks and run them "into the ground." Only then should new vehicles be acquired
- You could write off more through depreciation than you could with leasing over the first year
- Trade-in value is the same whether you lease or buy
- Leasing lets you turn in the vehicle at the end of the term and either walk away, purchase the vehicle at a predetermined residual value, or arrange another lease
- Buy and you may increase the debt on your books. Lease, you pay as you go

Lease/Buy Scenario: **Report outline**

A	***Situation***
B	***Financial considerations***
B-1	Tight 6 month cash flow
B-2	Need cash flexibility
B-3	Capital for land acquisition
B-4	Importance of timing
B-5	Spreadsheet analysis
C	***Vehicles***
C-1	Increased usage
C-2/3	Greatest increase—HD vehicles
C-4	High maintenance—HD vehicles
C-5	Low trade-in value—HD vehicles
C-6/7	Less increase—LD vehicles
C-8	Good trade in value—LD vehicles
D	***Purchase***
D-1	High usage HD vehicles
D-2	Delay—run HD into ground
E	***Lease***
E-1	Better for lower use vehicles
E-2	Monthly lease more than loan
E-3	Flexible—does not tie up capital
E-4	New vehicle every 2-3 years
E-5	More vehicle for the money
F/F-1	***Finance: bank versus dealership***
F-2	Equal cost
F-3	Prefer relationship with bank or dealership?

Conclusions

Recommendations

Structuring an outline to write your report

What any method of analysis must do is give you the structure, or outline, to write your report. The outline for the Lease/Buy Scenario is derived from the key points identified in the previous two pages. Following the A through F elements set out on the page opposite, allows you to fully discuss what you have found:

A—deals with the current situation, the terms of reference, plus any background information

B—deals with the number one issue—the company's financial situation. The director of finance must have flexibility, given the company's cash flow situation over the next six months and its commitment to purchase land

C—deals with vehicles—their condition, their maintenance costs, trade-in values and increased future usage

D & E—the factors to consider when deciding whether to lease or buy and how usage affects that decision

F—finance costs are about the same, whether going through the bank or the dealership. The question then becomes, is it more important to the company to cultivate its relationship with the bank or the dealership?

Next steps

Once you have all these elements in place, you have a solid basis on which to develop your conclusions and make recommendations. This now allows you to begin assembling and writing your report.

The writing steps

- Format
- Outline
- First draft
- Rework first draft
- Second draft
- Review second draft
- Final draft
- Executive summary
- Cover letter to the report

Lease/Buy Scenario: **Format**

This is a short report. It will likely contain the following:

- Cover letter
- Cover page
- Executive summary
- Terms of reference/background/methodology
- Main body of report—research, analysis, spreadsheets
- Conclusions
- Recommendations
- Resources/bibliography—people spoken with, articles read, web sites used

IV - WRITING THE REPORT

It's time to commit your thoughts and findings to paper. Here's the likely series of steps you must take:

- Decide on the format (incorporates your outline)
- Write a first draft
- Rework the draft for content
- Review this new (second) draft. Revise for any content and edit for style, tone and manner
- Review this final draft, then write the executive summary and/or cover letter. Make any last-minute corrections before going to print

What format will you use?

The format may include all or some of the following:

1. ***Cover page***
   Contains title, requester, author/s, date
2. ***Acknowledgments*** (optional)
   Identifies and thanks those who contributed to the report
3. ***Table of contents*** (optional on short reports)
   Lists the report's contents and where to find them
4. ***Executive summary*** (optional on short reports)
   Summary of key facts, conclusions and recommendations
5. ***Terms of reference/Introduction***
   Purpose of report, terms of reference, background material
6. ***Methodology & procedures***
   Usually incorporated into the introduction
7. ***Main body of report***
   Complete discussion of the report, with emphasis on the research conducted and the analysis of that research
8. ***Conclusions***
   The author's conclusions
9. ***Recommendations***
   Best options to achieve the objectives
10. ***Appendices*** (optional)
    Useful information not required in the body of the report
11. ***Bibliography***
    A listing of sources consulted for the report
12. ***Glossary*** (optional)
    Unfamiliar terms defined; e.g., technical, medical
13. ***Index*** (optional)
    Usually only in a major report

First Draft

- Focus on the report's purpose
- Space on the page:
  - two or three inch margin
  - double or triple spacing

Lease/Buy Scenario: **Introduction**

Why this report is needed

This report has been requested by the management of Goertz Construction & Development Inc. Its purpose is to determine whether to lease or finance the replacement of six pick-up trucks (four light duty, two heavy duty) over the next 6-12 months. Management would appreciate seeing a variety of options, based on the best use of funds and/or continuing to use present vehicles for a longer time.

Preserving cash flow is critical

In preparing this report we were asked to pay special attention to the cash flow requirements of the company, particularly over the next six months, and how that would impact the buy or lease decision. Another factor that might influence the decision is expected growth of the company in the 6 month to 18 month time frame. During that time vehicle usage is expected to increase substantially.

Some important background factors

While gathering information for this report, we were told that the company is intent on improving its image and that having new trucks every two or three years was a factor. However, with any vehicles of this nature, the key was functionality. These are working vehicles and that is the main criteria in their purchase.

Why we must have the statistics on vehicle usage

We decided that the up-front information we needed was usage, since decisions to lease or buy vehicles is highly dependent on usage. We also decided that we needed to have a clear handle on the company's cash flow projections as well as an impending decision to purchase land for development. These steps would be taken before we approached either a truck dealership or the company's financial institution to discuss buy or lease options with industry professionals.

WRITING THE FIRST DRAFT

Some practical instructions

1. As you write, *check that everything you do is focused towards the objective of the report*. Keep your purpose statement in front of you at all times.
2. Give yourself space on each page to work with. I like at least a three inch margin on the left, and I'll sometimes use double spacing. This allows me to rewrite/add/edit easily in that margin. (Some people prefer single or triple spacing—whatever works for you.)*
3. Unless it is a highly technical report, perhaps the most important issue is to ***keep your report very readable***.

Incorporate the outline into the format

The foot of page 180 indicates the format for the Lease/Buy Scenario. Short analytical reports will likely follow a similar format. The outline you develop (from a mind map or a skeleton plan) fits easily into this format. For example, from the Lease/Buy Scenario:

- A (Situation) covers terms of reference, background & methodology
- B through F constitute the main body of the report
- Conclusions and recommendations follow logically

Write the introductory section

You explain why the report is being written, followed by the scope of the report—its terms of reference. Remember to include any background information that you've been told about or discover in your research. With the Lease/Buy Scenario, the acquisition of land for development was very important background information since it affects cash flow.

You also include in this introduction a brief section on your research and how you obtained the information. This leads you into the body of the report as set up in your outline.

**Due to space limitations we have used single spacing in the Lease/Buy Scenario examples in order to show more content.*

Lease/Buy Scenario
Excerpt from research/analysis

The cash flow situation

Generally speaking, the company's financial situation is moving ahead well. Ongoing development contracts provide for a steady income flow for the next quarter. It then slows for a couple of months and picks up with the major development of the Transhill site at the eastern boundary of the city. Transhill has the potential to substantially boost company profitability – but not for a further six months. In between the company is faced with:

- Acquisition costs of development land
- Infrastructure payment to the city for the Transhill site

These payments, essential for the future growth of Goertz Construction, will severely limit the funds available for major outlays above and beyond normal expenses. In considering the options as to whether to lease or buy, or simply maintain the vehicles, this cash flow is a critical factor.

What are the vehicles going to cost us to maintain?

We posed the question "What are the costs of maintenance likely to be, given the age of the vehicles and their expected usage?" We found that:

- The two heavy duty trucks, 7 and 8 years old respectively, are showing increased wear and costs to maintain
- Usage will only increase with new projects coming on line
- Their trade-in value is low
- The light duty vehicles, two 4 years old and two 6 years old are seeing additional maintenance costs, but in line with expectations. Despite considerable usage, their trade-in value remains high

We had lengthy discussions with maintenance and finance about all these vehicles. In particular we discussed the costs of maintaining the heavy duty trucks, particularly with increased usage.

The issue of replacement

We investigated the costs of replacing these vehicles, either by lease or by purchase. We found that the monthly lease costs for the amount of use was prohibitively high. Purchasing the vehicle new, though a high cost, would allow the company to depreciate the vehicle quickly in the first few years, and provide potential tax savings.

Given the company's cash flow over the next six months, the question up for discussion is whether it remains less costly to maintain these vehicles for the time being, than purchase new ones once cash flow improves.

Write the main sections

Make good use of your outline

Use your outline to sequence the main body of your report. Make sure that the outline is laid out so that each issue is discussed in turn, the most important issue being dealt with first. The others will then follow in descending order of importance. You will note from the Lease/Buy Scenario research/analysis opposite how the most important issue for discussion—the company's cash flow situation—comes first, followed by a conversation regarding the vehicles, their maintenance costs, usage and trade-in values.

Use headlines to focus audience attention

Headlines focus the audience's attention on the discussion. These headlines help not just at the start of a section, but in any important subsections as well.

Use paragraphs effectively

Expect to use at least one paragraph to introduce the section itself and separate paragraphs for each major point. Of course you can also use bullets effectively to more succinctly make your points. You present the information you've uncovered, discuss it, analyze it and finally draw conclusions from it.

Flow in your discussion

The points in one section should bridge from one paragraph to another:

> *The first sentence in a paragraph introduces the second. The second refers back to the first and introduces the third and so on. These sentences provide full or sustained development. It's like a knit pattern. If it doesn't connect, it will unravel and the reader won't be able to progress "with you." (You want the reader to follow what you've said and understand it the first time around, easily.) Finally you have a sentence, or sentences, which create "closure" for that paragraph as well as being the hook to the next paragraph and a bridge or transition to the next idea/concept.*
>
> Ten Steps to Help You Write
> Better Essays & Term Papers (p.105)

Conclusions (first draft)

- Built step by step from key points
- What 2-3 points do you want your reader to remember?

Lease/Buy Scenario: **First draft conclusions**

We have come up with a number of conclusions from our conversations with company staff and other professionals. The most important consideration we were faced with was the company's cash flow situation over the next six months. Time and again we were reminded that to meet its regular obligations, cover additional costs of land acquisition and infrastructure, the cash flow had to be carefully channeled.

Vehicle costs, both maintenance and acquisition, impact cash flow. We came to the conclusion that it might be better for the present to continue to absorb high maintenance costs, especially on the two heavy duty vehicles, rather than incur either lease or purchase costs.

In terms of whether to lease or purchase new vehicles, mileage plus type of usage were determining factors. The higher the usage, the better choice was to buy. The lower the usage, the greater the advantage for leasing. The regular duty vehicles not only fit that characteristic, but because their trade-in value remains high, action should be taken soon. In terms of whether to use the bank or dealer to lease or buy, we found that costs were fairly even.

We did discover that the company wanted to build its image. On that basis we concluded that leasing would provide a new vehicle every 2 to 3 years. As well, the company would be able to lease a better quality vehicle for the money.

Recommendations (first draft)

Lease/Buy Scenario: **First draft recommendations**

Based on the conclusions from our research, the contributions of others, and spreadsheet analysis, our preferred option is as follows:

1. Pay close attention to cash flow so as to decide when to acquire new regular duty vehicles
2. Within 8 months trade in the two oldest light duty vehicles and lease two new ones. This will allow you good trade-in value and a reasonable lease rate in return
3. Maintain the other two newer light duty vehicles for at least 18 months before trading them in to lease new vehicles. That will place them on a regular rotation of serviceable vehicles and keep maintenance to a minimum
4. Maintain the heavy duty vehicles as long as possible and replace by purchase when feasible
5. Lease through dealership to maintain existing relationships

Save any self-editing till later

This is the first draft of your report. Don't edit yourself at this stage—just let the writing flow. Too much editing impedes flow and tends to hinder progress. It's more important to get the facts and analysis on paper. Don't worry if you write too much. You can always revise or edit later.

Write your conclusions and recommendations

Your conclusions

You have completed your analysis of the situation. It's time to write your conclusions. These are built step by step on the results that came from each key point you considered. Focus on the two to three points that you want your audience to remember—that's because as listeners or readers, we tend only to remember two to three pieces of information. You don't leave out the other points you wish to make—it's simply placing emphasis on those that are the most important.

Your recommendations

Recommendations come from the conclusions. Write them up in such a way that they flow from your conclusions and provide a clear pathway for the reader to come to a decision. The recommendations should be sharp and focused, using action words for greatest impact.

Review and rework the first draft

- Edit primarily for content

Lease/Buy Scenario:

Reworking first draft—conclusions

We have come up with a number of conclusions from our conversations with company staff and other professionals. The most important consideration we were faced with was the company's cash flow situation over the next six months. Time and again we were reminded that to meet its regular obligations, cover additional costs of land acquisition and infrastructure, the cash flow had to be carefully channeled.

Vehicle costs, both maintenance and acquisition, impact cash flow. We came to the conclusion that it might be better for the present to continue to absorb high maintenance costs, especially on the two heavy duty vehicles, than incur either lease or purchase costs.

In terms of whether to lease or purchase new vehicles, mileage plus type of usage were determining factors. The higher the usage, the better to buy. The lower the usage, the more advantage for leasing. The regular duty vehicles not only fit that characteristic, but because their trade-in value remains high, action should be taken soon. In terms of whether to use the bank or dealership to lease or buy, we found that costs were fairly even.

We did discover that the company wanted to build its image. On that basis we concluded that leasing would provide a new vehicle every 2-3 years – where the company could get a better value vehicle for the money.

REVIEWING THE FIRST DRAFT

You have a first draft in your hands. No doubt it's tempting to say a few things about the toil and sweat it took you to get there. In practical terms, however, you need to take a close look at what you've got. Before you do, unless you're pressured by deadlines, set the draft aside for a while—preferably a day or two. When you return to it you can look at it with fresh eyes. You may also want to pass this draft to colleagues to obtain their feedback.

Pay particular attention to content

In reviewing the first draft, content editing is the most important task. Is the report complete? Is it accurate? Is anything missing? What's there that should not be there? As you go through your draft, mark where major reworking or additional input is required, or where something needs to be deleted.

Next, try a second read through, this time checking from your readers' point of view. What do they see? Can they follow what you're saying? Do they have the information on which to make a decision?

Reworking the draft

Once you've finished reviewing, you probably have several corrections. Sections are circled, arrows redirect words and sentences, and you may have plenty of question marks. There might also be feedback from colleagues, which you could incorporate into the next version if applicable. On the opposite page is a reworking of the draft on conclusions from page 186. This reworking is incorporated into the second draft excerpt on page 190.

Try working in chunks

Everyone has different ways of reworking a text. If you have problems you might like to try working in chunks. A chunk can be an introductory section consisting of several paragraphs. It might be three or four pages. Sometimes it's a single paragraph that's not quite right.

My practice is to work each chunk intensively until I'm satisfied that what I've written is on the mark, or at least close, before moving on. Sometimes I'll find areas that need very little work. At other times changes can be substantial. This reworking leads to a second draft.

Second draft

- Recheck content
- Edit for style, tone, word choice

Lease/Buy Scenario: **Second draft—conclusions**

Any decision must meet cash flow requirements

From our research, background information, and consultations with company staff and other professionals, we have come up with a number of conclusions. Without question the most important is the company's cash flow requirements over the next six months. Time and again we were reminded that to meet its regular obligations and cover additional costs of land acquisition and infrastructure, cash flow had to be carefully channeled. Clearly, the question of leasing or purchasing new vehicles must satisfy this requirement.

Maintain heavy duty vehicles as long as possible

We concluded that it might be better for the company to continue maintaining their vehicles, especially the two heavy duty vehicles, than incur either lease or purchase costs at this time, then make appropriate decisions when cash flow permits.

The greater the usage, the less the advantage of leasing

The most important consideration on whether to lease or purchase a new vehicle is usage:

- What kind of mileage is expected?
- What kind of application?

The higher the usage, the greater the cost to lease. The lower the usage, the more advantage for leasing. Our overall conclusion from looking closely at the data is that the light duty vehicles should be leased and the heavy duty vehicles, whose usage is already high and projected to get higher, should be purchased.

Replacement priorities

In terms of priorities, we concluded that the two oldest light duty trucks should be replaced first:

- They still have a high trade-in value
- Cash flow at six months can probably accommodate this

The other light duty trucks could be added to a lease rotation where the company would receive a new vehicle every year, supporting a requirement to improve corporate image.

That leaves the two heavy duty trucks. The general consensus, supported by spreadsheet analysis, is to maintain these vehicles until it is no longer cost effective, then purchase new or used.

REVIEWING THE SECOND DRAFT

Your editing now depends on how much content change occurred between the first and second drafts. The greater the impact on content, the more the edit focuses on getting content right first. The closer the content to what is required, the more the edit focuses on style, tone and manner.

Read the draft out loud

I recommend that you read the draft out loud. Does the overall report work? Does it flow? Is it focused? Have you repeated yourself? Is your tone consistent? Have you used inappropriate language or jargon? Have you used the KISS principle and kept the report simpler rather than complex?

How many drafts?

I've seen books on writing reports that say you'll need five or six drafts. My response is that if you've done a thorough analysis and structured your outline as completely as possible, there's no reason why two to three drafts won't do it. If I have to go beyond two or three drafts, I begin to wonder where I've gone wrong. I'll concede that if it's a particularly long report, with several parties participating, it may take five or six drafts.

On the page opposite you will see the second draft of the conclusions for the Lease/Buy Scenario. It may be fine as it is. It may require some fine tuning—but it's close to final.

FINAL DRAFT

Once you are satisfied that you have everything in place and final editing is done, you can complete your report with an executive summary and/or some kind of cover letter.

Executive summary

- The first page to which the reader turns
- Contains the essence and highlights of the report

Lease/Buy Scenario: **Executive summary (excerpt)**

<u>Situation</u>

Goertz Construction & Development must replace six vehicles over the next two years. This is a challenging time because of two main factors:

- The company's tight cash flow situation over the next 6 months
- The demands of a growing business

<u>The impact of cash flow</u>

Analysis of the cash flow situation indicates high demand for flexibility over the next 6-12 months. Since the company needs to keep its borrowing costs down and revenues from developments are not expected until later in the third quarter, delaying major purchases until absolutely necessary is critical.

<u>The impact of a growing business</u>

The company has made commitments to its future success, such as the acquisition of new land. Now it's in a cash crunch because the work has to be done on current properties before significant returns come on stream. In terms of equipment, that means company vehicles will be in heavy demand, with limited cash resources to start replacing them.

<u>The vehicle dilemma—lease or buy—and when?</u>

Tight cash flow and heavy vehicle usage are a tough combination. The company cannot afford to replace today, or even in six months. Yet, the vehicles must be maintained as their usage increases, a major cost requirement.

Usage is a key determinant of whether to lease or buy. The greater the usage, the higher the leasing cost. We concluded that vehicles with the lowest usage, the four light duty pick-ups, should be leased. Done on a staged basis over the next year and a half, it will allow regular replacement and always provide the company with new vehicles.

The heavy duty vehicles have and will continue to have the greatest usage. In our view, these two heavy duty units, with their greater usage, should be purchased. Details on how and when this should be done are set out in the recommendations.

Cover letter

- Accompanies report
- May touch on major findings
- Can take the place of an executive summary in short reports

Executive summary

Without question, the executive summary is the first page to which the reader will turn. There may even be enough information on that page for the reader not to bother with reading the rest of the report.

The executive summary is where you pull all the key elements of your report together in one tight package. This allows the reader to very quickly go through the essence of the report—what the purpose was, what research you did, your conclusions and your recommendations.

Write the executive summary once you are satisfied that the other components of the report are in final shape. Your reader expects the executive summary to be concise, clear and focused on the report's objective. It must flow smoothly and justifiably from introduction to recommendations. In terms of length, it is usually no more than a page, maybe two.

With shorter reports, the executive summary can be incorporated into the cover letter to the report.

An executive summary to the owner of Goertz Construction & Development—the Lease/Buy Scenario—is shown on the page opposite.

The cover letter

The cover letter accompanies the report, stating that the report is complete and perhaps touching on major findings. It may also take the place of the executive summary. As well, the cover letter might serve to set up a presentation of the report to an organization, committee, or executive.

Next steps

Content is one thing. The packaging of content is another. Accurate content is invariably helped by good packaging. Poor packaging can damage your written efforts.

Packaging the report

Presentation in person or written report only? This decision affects design.

Good visuals can create great impressions

- Graphics
- Photographs
- Tables
- Charts
- Use of color

Readability

- Use bullet points
- Keep sentences shorter
- Keep column narrow
- White space

BUT REMEMBER

Accuracy of content is paramount.

V - PACKAGING THE REPORT

How will your report be presented?

If you want to create a great first impression, then packaging can play an important part. One determinant of packaging is how the report will be presented. Will it be in person or as a written report only?

Delivered in person

If you are delivering in person, you may find that you use more bullet points in your text as you are able to provide a full verbal explanation to back up these points. Visually you may also use more graphics, photographs and other aids. However, regardless of your delivery, the report must be sufficiently complete that it will stand on its own, able to be read and understood by those not at the presentation.

Written report only

Submitting a written report, without delivering it in person, doesn't mean not using bullets. It does mean that your explanations will need to be more complete and bullets may not be appropriate. You can enhance your report with the use of various fonts, shading, outlining, graphics, photos and figures. For example, the Lease/Buy Scenario will make use of spreadsheets to show cost options more effectively than simply using figures in the text.

Make the report more readable

I have a coffee table book on Broadway musicals. It's beautifully illustrated. The writing, though, is spread across a page that is at least ten inches wide. That width does not make for easy reading. Readability focuses on:

- Using bullet points
- Keeping sentences short and to the point
- Keeping the vertical column narrow
- Using white space–pages don't feel crammed and it's often easier to focus on and absorb the material

Caveat: content is paramount

I've seen great looking reports whose quality of content was far short of their appearance. I've also seen first rate content presented in a fashion that failed to represent the quality of the report. I believe that content is paramount. If the content doesn't work, no amount of glossing it up will improve it.

Writing considerations

Be objective

Handling writer's block

- Start with the introduction
- Jump in anywhere you feel confident
- Write in rough
- Take a break
- Give yourself a deadline
- Talk to someone

VI - WRITING CONSIDERATIONS

Be objective

Your report needs to be free of bias and editorializing. Just because a particular piece of information doesn't fit with your views, don't omit it. If you're giving your opinion, be sure that the reader realizes this. The audience needs to know that they are seeing all the facts and opinions, whether they agree with you or not.

Handling writer's block

Start with the introduction. You know why the report is being written, what the terms of reference are, and the research you had to carry out. But what if you've done the introduction and you want to start the body of the report? Many writers think they must start at the beginning and work their way through the report step by step. If this is how you think, break the rules!

• *Jump in anywhere you feel confident*
If you're stuck at the beginning of the report's main body, jump into a section that you know and write about that. It doesn't matter as long as you write—as long as you get a sense of accomplishment that you're getting it done. Then, when you're ready—go back and write from the beginning.

• *Write in rough*
Simply write in any area to get yourself going. You can adapt it or edit it later.

• *Take a break*
As suggested in other parts of this book, take a break. It can help you come back refreshed to the writing.

• *Give yourself a deadline*
One thing that can produce results is a deadline. I can't tell you the number of times I've written something under the pressure of a deadline and wonder where the idea, or the phrasing, came from. But it did, and it worked.

• *Talk to someone*
Another person may be able to guide you past the problem.

Appendix

Comparative MLA/APA referencing

MLA

General Rules

With the author, MLA lists the last name and first name as follows:

```
Rankine, Jerry.
```

[Use initials if first name not known]

With the title, MLA capitalizes the first letter of major words and proper nouns.

```
The Other Side of Midnight.
```

With the date:

- MLA places the date at the end, or next to the end
- May, June & July are spelled in full. Abbreviate all others: e.g. Dec. Sept.
- The date sequence is day month year with no commas:

  ```
  1 Apr. 2004
  ```

With the place of publication, unless the city is well known - e.g. Philadelphia - add the state or province (abbreviated - AK, CA, BC, NY), or name of the country.

If references overlap a line, indent each additional line by 5 spaces or 1/2 inch.

Books

- Last name, first name of author.
- Title.
- Place of publication: publisher, year of publication.

```
Gallwey, Timothy. The Inner Game of Work. London: Orion
     Business Books, 2000.
```

APA

General Rules

With the author, APA lists the last name followed by initial(s).

`Rankine, J.V.`

With the title, APA capitalizes only the first letter of the first word, proper nouns and the first word after a colon.

`The other side of midnight.`

With the date:

- APA always places the date of publication second, in parentheses after the author's name.
- Months are spelled in full - i.e. April, December
- The date sequence is generally year, month day:

  `2004, April 1`
- If no date is available, write: (n.d.).

With the place of publication, unless the city is well known - e.g. Philadelphia - add the state or province (abbreviated - AK, CA, BC, NY), or name of the country.

If references overlap a line, indent each additional line by 5 spaces or 1/2 inch.

Books

- Last name, initial(s) of author.
- (Year of publication).
- *Title.*
- Place of publication: publisher.

Gallwey, T. (2000). *The inner game of work.* London: Orion Business Books.

MLA

More than one author:

- For first author: Name, first name,
- For additional authors: first name last name, (*normally use comma before "and" if there are three authors*)
- Use "and" in full

Kyosaki, Robert and Sharon Lechter. Rich Dad, Poor Dad. Etc...

More than three authors:

- First named author is listed followed by "et al." ("et al." refers to the Latin "and others"). If there were a fourth author to Rich Dad, Poor Dad, the reference would begin:

Kyosaki, Robert, et al.

Journals/periodicals

- Last name, first name of author.
- "Title of article."
- Name of publisher/publication:
  a. Monthly magazine: Publisher/publication.
  b. Weekly magazine & newspaper: Publisher/publication (no period)
  c. Journal paginated by volume/issue: Publisher/publication volume #. issue # (e.g. Volume 22 Issue 7 = 22.7)
- Date:
  a. Monthly magazine: Month year:
  b. Weekly magazine & newspaper: Day month year:
  c. Journal paginated by volume/issue: (Year):
- Page #s: 333-334.

Article in a monthly magazine

Slywotzky, Adrian and Richard Wise. "Double-Digit Growth in No-Growth Times." Fast Company. Apr. 2003: 66-72.

APA

More than one author:

- Name, initial(s)., separated by commas.
- Use "&" abbreviation instead of the word "and"

Kiyosaki, R.T., & Lechter, S.L. (1998). *Rich dad poor dad*. Etc...

More than three authors:

- All author names are listed unless there are six or more when it would go to:

Kiyosaki, R.T., et al.

Journals/periodicals

- Last name, initial(s) of author.
- Date:
  a. Monthly magazine: (Year, month).
  b. Weekly magazine & newspaper: (Year, month day).
  c. Journal paginated by volume/issue: (Year).
- Title of article.
- Name of publisher/publication:
  a. Monthly/weekly magazine and newspaper: *Publisher/publication,* [Note: comma italicized]
  b. Journal paginated by volume/issue: *Publisher/publication, volume #* (issue #), (e.g. Volume 22 Issue 7 = 22 (7),) [Note: italicize only volume number, not issue number]
- Page #s: 333-334.
  [Except for newspapers & magazines, in which case the page numbers in your reference are preceded by 'p.' or 'pp.']

Article in a monthly magazine

Slywotzky, A., & Wise R. (2003, April). Double-digit growth in no-growth times. *Fast Company*, pp. 66-72.

MLA

Article in a weekly magazine

Greenlees, Donald. "Korea Eyes a New Track Record." Far Eastern Economic Review 1 Apr. 2004: 32-34.

Article in a newspaper

Robinson, Allan. "Bonds Slide as Interest Rate Increases Loom." The Globe and Mail 11 June 2004: B9.

Video

View from the Typewriter. Prod. Robert Duncan, George Johnson. National Film Board of Canada, 1993.

DVD

Powerboat Navigation with John Rousmaniere. Prod. Creative Programming Inc., Arnold Levin Productions. Bennett Marine Video, 2003.

Motion Picture

Lost in Translation. Dir. Sofia Coppola. Prods. Sofia Coppola and Ross Katz. Focus Features, 2003.

Personal interview

- Last name, first name.
- Type of communication.
- Date: Day month year.
- Each section is separated by periods.

Warren, Margaret. Personal Interview on Publisher Innovations at Chicago's O'Hare International Airport. 7 June 2004.

APA

Article in a weekly magazine

Greenlees, D. (2004, April 1). Korea eyes a new track record. *Far Eastern Economic Review*, pp. 32-34.

Article in a newspaper

Robinson, A. (2004, June 11). Bonds slide as interest rate increases loom. *The Globe and Mail*, p. B9.

Video

Duncan, R. & Johnson, G. (Producers). (1993). *View from the typewriter* [Videorecording]. Montreal, PQ: National Film Board of Canada.

DVD

Creative Programming Inc. & Arnold Levin Productions (Producers). (2003). *Powerboat Navigation with John Rousmaniere* [DVD]. Los Angeles: Bennett Marine Video.

Motion Picture

Coppola, S. & Katz, R. (Producers), & Coppola, S. (Director). (2003). *Lost in translation* [Motion picture]. United States: Focus Features.

Personal interview

The APA Manual states that personal communications, such as an interview, should be cited in text only.

MLA

A World Wide Web site

Include as much of the following as possible:
- Name of author, editor, compiler, etc., (if known): Last name, first name.
- "Title of document or portion." (If relevant)
- Title of web site.
- Date of web site, if known—or latest update: day month year.
- Name of any institution/organization sponsoring the site.
- Date of access: day month year
- <URL>. [Note: period at end of URL]

"How Do Energy Subsidies Distort the Energy Market?" Wind Energy. 21 Jul. 2004. American Wind Energy Association. 27 Jul. 2004. <http://www.awea.org/faq/subsidi.html>.

E-mail

- Name of originator: last name, first name.
- Title of communication, if available:
  a. "Subject line from posting," or,
  b. "Description of document."
- E-mail to recipient.
- Date: day month year.

Sawers, Neil. "Software Applications." E-mail to Peter Zavitz. 28 Nov. 2003.

APA

A World Wide Web site

Include as much of the following as possible:

- Name of author, editor, compiler, etc., (if known): Last name, initial(s).
- Date of web site, if known - or latest update. (Month day, year).
- Title of document or portion (if relevant). *
- *Title of web site.*
- Retrieval statement including date of access - month day, year - and URL [Note: change in date sequence + no period at end of URL]
- Where possible keep the URL on one line or break it in a logical place

How do energy subsidies distort the energy market? (2004, July 21). *Wind Energy*. Retrieved July 27, 2004, from http://www.awea.org/faq/subsidi.html

* If author not known, open with title, followed by date.

E-mail

APA requires personal communications, such as E-mails, to be cited in text only since they do not provide recoverable data.

REFERENCE MATERIAL

APA. Publication Manual of the American Psychological Association. 5th ed. Washington: American Psychological Association, 2001.

APA. APA Style. 2004. American Psychological Association. http://www.apastyle.org

Buzan, Tony. Head First. London: Thorsons, 2000.

Buzan, Tony. Use Your Head. Rev ed. London: BBC Books, 1998.

Buzan, Tony and Barry Buzan. The Mind Map Book. Rev ed. London: BBC Books, 1995.

Covey, Stephen, R. The 7 Habits of Highly Effective People. New York: Fireside/Simon & Schuster, 1990.

Gibaldi, Joseph. MLA Handbook for Writers of Research Papers. 6th ed. New York: The Modern Language Association of America, 2003.

Klauser, Henriette Anne. Writing on Both Sides of the Brain. San Francisco: Harper, 1987.

MLA. MLA Style. 2004. Modern Language Association. http://www.mla.org

Rico, Gabriele. Writing the Natural Way. Los Angeles: Jeremy P. Tarcher Inc., 1983.

Sawers, Neil. Ten Steps to Help You Write Better Essays & Term Papers. 3rd ed. Updated APA Version. Edmonton: The NS Group, 2002.

NOTES